The MEJT System

A New Tool for Day Trading the S&P 500 Index

By Jeffrey Tennant, MD

HARRIMAN HOUSE LTD

3A Penns Road
Petersfield
Hampshire
GU32 2EW
GREAT BRITAIN

Tel: +44 (0)1730 233870
Fax: +44 (0)1730 233880
Email: enquiries@harriman-house.com
Website: www.harriman-house.com

First published in Great Britain in 2011 by Harriman House

ISBN: 978-0-857190-35-2

British Library Cataloguing in Publication Data
A CIP catalogue record for this book can be obtained from the British Library.

Printed and bound in the UK by MPG Books Group.

Contents

Preface

What this book covers

This book describes the MEJT system, which I have used for over eight years to help me trade the Standard and Poor's 500 index (S&P 500). The system identifies which moves have staying power and which moves do not. It also helps one establish price targets at which support and resistance can be expected to occur. The system is different from any I have seen on the market.

It is important to see the MEJT system as an addition to the arsenal of the technical analyst. Though the system has very useful predictive qualities, it should never be used in isolation. Use it along with other tools of market analysis.

Whom this book is for

The MEJT system is designed for use by experienced day traders who are already familiar with technical analysis of the stock market and who wish to add another tool to their trading methodologies. Since the system is used exclusively with the S&P 500, this book will be of use mainly to those who day trade this index.

How this book is structured

After an introductory chapter explaining how the MEJT system came about and its basic principles, each chapter in this book lays out a set of rules. These rules are followed by a number of examples in which the rules are applied. The final chapter – chapter 9 – is composed of trading examples only. Chapter 9 is designed so that people who want to skip ahead to the back of the book will, in many cases, be able to deduce what the rules of the system are even though the rules are not stated explicitly in this chapter.

In most cases, trading examples in this book are named simply with an example number and illustrative figures are labelled with just the date from which the respective price chart is taken. I have deliberately omitted more descriptive labels to allow readers to think about the charts and to use the MEJT rules to make a prediction, before reading my own analysis of the situation.

Part 1

Introduction

1

The MEJT System: Background, Definitions and General Principles

Introduction

Kudzu is a plant which grows in many places. It is native to Japan and China but has made an effortless transition to the United States, where it has proliferated so much that it is known as the vine that ate the South.

Most technical analysis techniques are like kudzu. They flourish everywhere. Bollinger bands and moving averages may have been developed for the stock market, but they work for commodities and futures as well. Stock traders also routinely use these and other indicators to trade the Forex market. When a new security or a new market begins trading, technical analysts use techniques they have used with other issues to analyse it. If something trades, market technicians can analyse it using techniques they already have.

The Haleakala silversword is not like kudzu. It is a beautiful plant which grows in a highly restricted range in Haleakala National Park on the Island of Maui. Move it outside of its narrow ecological niche and it dies. That pretty much describes the MEJT system I use to help me trade the S&P 500. It doesn't work for individual stocks, for other indices, commodities, Forex or anything else. But for the S&P 500 it is a very useful tool. Like the Haleakala silversword, give the MEJT system the right environment and it blossoms.

The uses of the MEJT system

The system's main use is to help one day trade the S&P 500. However, less frequently, it can help one make long-term predictions.

- In March 2003 a multi-year rally in stocks began. MEJT predicted that, ultimately, all of the gain would retrace.

- In October 2007 the market made a major top. MEJT predicted, soon after the top, that the S&P 500 was going to circle the drain for a long time.

- And, as far as short-term calls are concerned, take a look at Figure 1.

Figure 1 – S&P 500 28-29 October 2009

There was a big drop on 28 October 2009. MEJT predicted, well in advance, that the drop would retrace, most likely before a little over a trading day had passed.

Basic principles of the MEJT system

The fundamental principle of the MEJT system is that market action during certain times of the day has predictive power over future price action. Were it not for the internet, I might never have learned that.

In early 2002 a member of an internet chat room acquainted me with the characteristics of the five-minute bar beginning at 9:05am Central Time (CT). He said that another trader had discovered that, if the market were to trend sustainably during the morning (and perhaps during the day) its retraces, if any, would not go through this bar. This is the bar I call **am MEJT**, or **am** for short. Unbeknownst to me, the person who had discovered this fact had developed an entire trading system based on it. Perhaps it was just as well that his system was unknown to me; his system turned out to be totally different to mine and I think mine is superior.

The am sequence

The sponsor of the same chat room routinely made a prediction for the day's action at 9:15am CT, five minutes after the **am** bar printed. I thought there must be something special about the bar after **am** MEJT as well. It soon became obvious that, while those bars were important, it was the following bar (the five-minute bar beginning at 9:15 CT) that had the most predictive power.

I define the three five-minute bars beginning at 9:05am CT as **am MEJT**, **am MEJT+1** and **am MEJT+2**; for short I usually refer to them as **am**, **am+1** and **am+2**. The three bars as a whole are called the *am pattern* or *am sequence*.

The basic principles of the am sequence are these:

- In general, the **am** bar is the default reference bar. Attempts to trend, if sustainable, should not correct through this bar. Under some conditions the reference bar changes.

- The action of the **am+1** and **am+2** bars determines whether there will be an attempt to trend.

- The action of the **am+2** bar determines whether or not the attempt to trend will succeed.

To be sustainable, any attempt to trend during the morning must show an attempt to trend (in the same direction) by the am+1 and **am+2** bars. In addition, action of the **am+2** bar must indicate that the attempt will succeed, i.e. that the attempt is sustainable. If the rules for sustainability are not met, prices should retrace to the reference bar. The specific rules are discussed in chapter 2.

Thinking about why the MEJT system works

I did not know why the system worked, but I had a theory. I assumed that, after the rush of public orders had been taken care of during the first 35 minutes of trading, big money players began to get down to business, and that they did so at a very consistent time. If the market trended strongly enough during that time, the trend could continue. If not, I felt there was no institutional support for the move and that prices would retrace back to the **am** bar. Whether or not that assumption was true, trading based on it proved profitable for me.

The MEJT sequence

Trading the am sequence proved so rewarding that I wondered if big money players had a similar consistent pattern of behaviour after they returned from lunch. Assuming they had

lunch in the Eastern Time Zone (ET), it did indeed appear that there was a similar pattern after lunch. Market action from 1:10-1:25pm ET (12:10-12:25pm CT) has predictive powers.

The three five-minute bars beginning at 12:10 CT are defined as **MEJT**, **MEJT+1** and **MEJT+2**. As a whole, they are referred to as the *pm pattern*, *pm sequence* or *MEJT sequence*.

The basic principles of the MEJT sequence are these:

- In general, the **MEJT** bar is the default reference bar. Under some conditions the reference bar changes.

- The action of the **MEJT+1** and **MEJT+2** bars determines whether there will be an attempt to trend.

- The action of the **MEJT+2** bar determines whether or not the attempt to trend will succeed.

The rules for trading these principles are similar to the rules for trading the am pattern, but there are some significant differences. For example, trending moves during the morning should not penetrate the am MEJT bar. During the afternoon, however, a slight penetration of the MEJT bar does not preclude a sustainable move. Furthermore, such a slight penetration is not rare. Also, prices predicted by the MEJT pattern are more likely to print within their preferred time frames.

To be sustainable, any attempt to trend during the afternoon must show an attempt to trend (in the same direction) by the **MEJT+1** and **MEJT+2** bars. In addition, action of the **MEJT+2** bar must indicate that the attempt will succeed. If the rules for sustainability are not met, prices should retrace to or through the reference bar. The specific rules are discussed in chapter 4.

Targets

When a MEJT signal is given, a target for ensuing price action is established. Different patterns have different targets, and these will be explained in the course of the text. In general, if the am sequence or the MEJT sequence indicates that an attempt to trend will succeed, a target is created either at a prior high, a prior low, at the prior day's close, or at a given price level. If the am sequence or the MEJT sequence indicate a trending attempt will not succeed, a target is created at or just past the reference bar of the sequence which made the prediction.

Targets will be discussed in detail in chapter 7.

Using TradeStation to identify the bars of the am sequence and MEJT sequence

Before discussing the rules of the systems, it is useful to have TradeStation identify the bars of the am sequence and the MEJT sequence for us. One can get a clearer picture by seeing the bars on one's computer than one can get from illustrations. In addition, one can identify prices by right-clicking over or under the price bars.

Open TradeStation. Then, on the tools menu on the left side of the page, go to <**easy language**>, click on <**new easy language document**> and scroll down to <**paint bar**>. Give the paint bar indicator a name, like <**paintMEJTbar**> and copy the program shown in Program Excerpt 1.

Program Excerpt 1

```
[LegacyColorValue = true];

Inputs: time1(0910), time2(0915),
time3(0920), time4(1215), time5(1220),
time6(1225);

if time = time1 or time = time2 or time =
time3 then

begin

Plot1(high, "5 min chart", yellow);

Plot2(low, "5 min chart", yellow);

end;

if time = time4 or time = time5 or time =
time6 then

begin

Plot1(high, "5 min chart", red);

Plot2(low, "5 min chart", red);

end;
```

Verify the program. Create a five-minute chart. Right-click on the chart and choose **<insert analysis technique>**. Open **<paintMEJTbar>** under the paint bar menu.

The program will paint the **am MEJT** sequence in yellow and the MEJT sequence in red for computers set for the CT zone.

All the charts in this book are in United States Central Time – those living in other time zones can change the times listed on the **<Inputs>** line in the program above. Those who live in states such as Hawaii or Arizona, which have no daylight savings time, or in countries whose daylight savings time changes on dates other than those used in the United States, will need to make adjustments. One option is to make a second paint bar indicator and to change things manually on the appropriate dates. When I lived in Arizona, I just left my computer on CT.

A word of caution here is that I cannot verify whether or not programs other than TradeStation will work. Specifically, I have tried programs which are available for free on the internet or at lower cost elsewhere. For some reason, the providers I tried had slightly different data than TradeStation's. When those data were used, the system did not work. Unlike many other indicators, slight changes in the data can have big consequences in the MEJT system's predictive ability. Think of it as like the Haleakala silversword: if the environment is changed just a little the plant will not grow.

Naming of the MEJT system

For the sake of completeness, I would like to go over the reason I named the system MEJT. The trader who originally discovered the bar I call **am MEJT** had a different name for it. When I discovered the pm pattern I named it MEJT with *ME* being borrowed from his name for the bar from the am pattern and *JT* being my initials. I have been asked not to use the name the other trader gave to the bar he discovered, but he says he is happy for me to use MEJT.

Part 2

Morning Signals

2

Trading the Am MEJT Sequence

Most of us have a daily schedule. So does the market.

Seasoned day traders of the S&P 500 know they have to be on their toes when the market opens; often it is a time of marked volatility which can extend for an hour or more. It may be the time a day-long trend begins. On other occasions, after the first hour, volatility tends to slow down. The lunch hour is usually not the time one looks for a big move to take place. The early afternoon has a reputation of dilly-dallying around unpredictably. Then the last hour of trading arrives and traders seeking action often have another shot.

What day traders may not know is that there are specific times during the day which act as harbingers for future price action on the S&P 500. This book identifies those times, shows you how they give their signals and demonstrates how to use that information. This chapter will look at how to trade the morning's predictive pattern – the **am MEJT** sequence.

First, let's define what we are talking about.

Defining the am sequence

- The **am MEJT** bar (**am** for short) is the five-minute bar beginning at 9:05am CT.

- The **am+1** bar is the next five-minute bar, beginning at 9:10am CT.

- The **am+2** bar is the subsequent five-minute bar, beginning at 9:15am CT.

These three bars collectively are known as the **am sequence** (as shown in Figure 2.1). The action of the **am** sequence enables us to arrive at the **am prediction**.

Figure 2.1 – The 3 bars of the am MEJT sequence 23 April 2010

The am prediction is often, but not always, satisfied during the morning in which the sequence prints (the morning is the part of the trading day before 10:45am CT). Most of the time, the prediction is satisfied within two trading days (which we refer to as the sequence's *preferred time*).

The *reference bar*, unless otherwise specified, is the **am** bar. If **am+1** has a higher high and a lower low than **am**, then **am+1** replaces **am** as the reference bar. If **am+2** has a higher high and a lower low than both **am** and **am+1**, then **am+2** becomes the reference bar (see Figure 2.2).

Figure 2.2 – 8 April 2010

The dotted yellow lines in Figure 2.2 show **am+1** has replaced **am** as the reference bar because it has a higher high and lower low.

- An **unsustainable trend** is one in which prices will return to the reference bar.

- A **sustainable trend** is one which need not revisit the reference bar. At some point its target should print.

Most of ones profits from trading the am prediction come from following sustainable trends. Reasonable profits can be made by fading the unsustainable trends.

Basic principle

The basic principle behind the am prediction is:

> The **am** bar is the standard reference bar. The actions of the **am+1** bar and the **am+2** bar determine whether or not the market will attempt to trend. The action of the **am+2** bar determines whether or not the attempt will succeed.

In order for a trend to be sustainable, all the criteria for sustainability must be met. Otherwise, the trend is marked as unsustainable and the S&P 500 will return to the reference bar.

Now is as good a point as any to lay down the rules.

Rules of the am sequence

- **In order for an am prediction to be generated, the day must have no unfilled gaps.**

Think of it this way: the principle is that the am sequence can forecast future price action because market movers reveal their intentions during that time. If the market has gapped and has held that gap, it is assumed that they have already shown their hands for that morning.

The chart from 8 April 2010 (Figure 2.2) has an unfilled gap. Although the am sequence still contains useful information under the MEJT rules (since the reference bar should not be violated if the morning is going to trend), it does not generate an am prediction.

Sometimes identifying an unfilled gap is not as easy as it seems. The reason is that all components of the S&P 500 do not open simultaneously. If one looks at printed prices only it is possible one would reach a different conclusion than that which would be reached if it all of the index's components opened at once. The way around this issue is to examine derivatives of the S&P 500. The exchange traded fund with the ticker symbol SPY (the SPDR S&P 500 ETF) will always reflect prices as if all its components opened together. So will S&P futures and E-mini contracts.

- **Am MEJT is the default reference bar.**

The reference bar acts as a support/resistance level which can remain significant for days, even after targets from the am prediction have printed. It can act as a support/resistance level even if there is no am prediction (because an unfilled gap is present). If **am+1** has a higher high and lower low than **am MEJT**, then it replaces it as the reference bar. If **am+2** has a higher high and lower low than both **am MEJT** and **am+1** then it becomes the reference bar.

- **The action of the am+1 bar and the am+2 bar determines whether or not the market will attempt to trend.**

In fact, the action of the **am+1** and **am+2** bars tends to mimic the subsequent action of the market itself. One assesses the action of these two bars by looking at their high to low ranges, their closes and their ability to escape the ranges of the bars which preceded them.

For example, if **am+2** has a higher high and higher low than **am+1**, the market is attempting to rally. If **am+2** has a lower high and lower low than **am+1**, the market is attempting to decline. If **am+2** closes within the range of **am MEJT**, there is no attempt to trend. If both **am+1** and **am+2** are unable to break outside of the **am** range, there is no attempt to trend and ensuing price action tends to have a narrow range (just like the **am+1** and **am+2** bars).

For a market to attempt to trend higher, **am+2** must have a higher high than **am+1**. It is not necessary for it to have a higher low. For a market to attempt to trend lower, **am+2** must have a lower low than **am+1**. It is not necessary for it to have a lower high.

Figure 2.3 – the am+1 and am+2 bars attempt a rally 5 January 2010

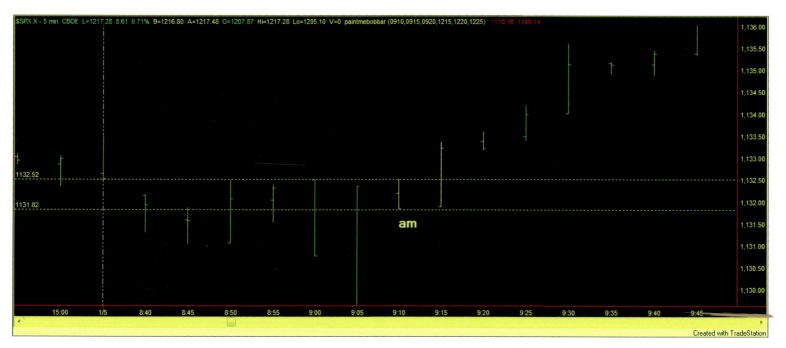

Figure 2.4 – the am+1 and am+2 bars do not attempt to trend as am+2 closes within the range of am MEJT 14 January 2010

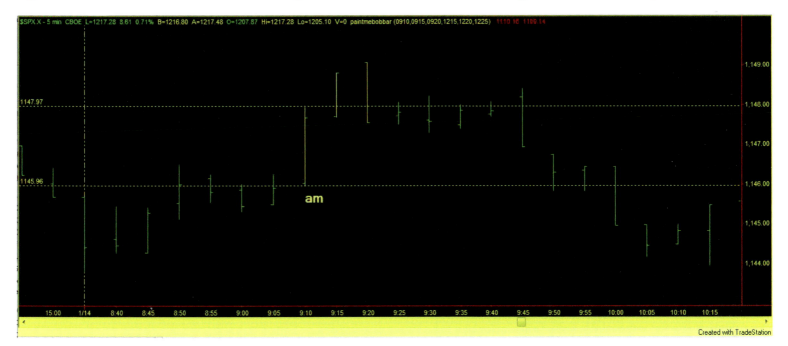

- **The action of the am+2 bar determines whether or not any attempt to trend will be sustainable.**

Since **am+2** determines whether a trend will be sustainable one may consider it, and not the **am MEJT** bar, as the most important bar of the am sequence. When a trend is strong and immediate, the **am+2** bar certainly gives us more information

than we get from either of the other two bars. Under this same circumstance of a strong trend, **am+1** gives us the next most information. The **am MEJT** bar itself usually adds very little.

Before looking more closely at how **am+2** determines whether the attempt to trend will be sustainable, two more terms have to be defined:

- An **immediate trend** is one which begins before the market passes through the reference bar. There is a 0.20 tolerance for this. For example, if S&P 500 is at 1000 and the am prediction is for a rally, then an immediate trend is one which begins before the market prints a price level under (not at) 999.80.

- A **delayed trend** is one which begins after the market passes through the reference bar.

Now that the rules have been defined let's look more closely at what the am *sequence shows us.*

Sustainable trends – the am+2 bar

In order for the three-bar am sequence to signify a sustainable trend, **am+2** must be a long bar, close in its distal (away from the **am** bar itself) half and take out a significant level.

Long, as in *long bar*, is a relative term. A bar 0.30 in length is too small. A bar 0.50 in length is long enough. However, the longer the bar and the further away from **am MEJT** the close, the better the ensuing trend if the trend is immediate. If the trend is delayed, the length of the bar and the distance of the close have no such predictive power.

By *take out a significant level* I mean the prior day's close or the extreme of the first 35 minutes of trading. For example, if **am+1** and **am+2** are trying to rally, then the prior day's close is one significant level and the high of the first 35 minutes of trading is another. If **am+1** and **am+2** are trying to decline, then the prior day's close and the low of the first 35 minutes of trading are the two significant levels.

Whether a move is immediate or delayed, the target of the move tends to print within two trading days. For example, if **am+2** completes at 9:20am on a Monday, the target is usually hit by 9:20am on Wednesday. If the target does not print within its preferred time, it is defined as a failed target. It is my belief that failed targets are actually postponed targets; they print eventually, although there is no time limit in which they are expected to do so.

In Figure 2.5 the **am+2** bar is long, closes in its upper half and takes out the prior day's close and the high of the first 35 minutes of trading. The am prediction is that a sustainable advance will occur, most likely within two days. When prices drop under the reference bar this indicates that the advance is delayed. The rules say the decline after the am sequence will not stick and that higher prices will print.

Figure 2.5 – am+1 and am+2 attempt a rally 6 January 2010

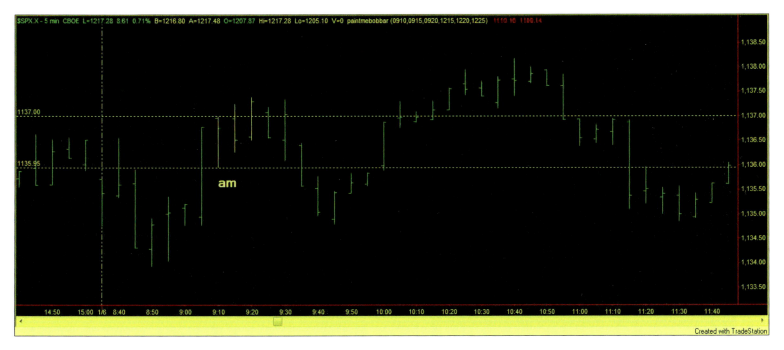

When a sustainable trend occurs before the market trades through the reference bar, the strength of the **am+1** and (to a greater extent) the **am+2** bars tends to mimic the strength of the trend which was signalled. The longer these bars and the farther away from **am MEJT** their closes, the more forceful the subsequent action of S&P 500 in the same direction. Strong action in the am sequence leads to strong action in the market if the move is immediate.

Figure 2.6 – am+1 and am+2 attempt a decline 12 November 2009

In Figure 2.6 the **am+1** and **am+2** bars are long and close at or near their lows; **am+2** takes out the significant level of the prior day's close. So long as the market does not go through the reference bar high, the elements are present for a strong decline. However, **am+2** did not take out the low of the first 35 minutes of trading. A move under that level before 10:45am is not sustainable, and S&P 500 should return to the reference bar, most likely within two days. As can be seen from Figure 2.6, it did.

How the strength of trends is indicated

Trends which are strong and immediate should be preceded by the appropriate am prediction. The most bearish am prediction would come if **am** was a long bar which closed at its low, **am+1** was a longer bar which closed at its low and **am+2** was the longest bar of all and closed at its low as well. Ideally, there would be little overlap between the bars, but such ideal situations hardly ever happen. The point to remember here is that a strong decline can ensue if these bars are declining strongly.

The most important move would be signalled by the **am+2** bar. An important move would be signalled by the **am+1** bar. And little information would be added by the **am** bar. (I cannot say no information would be added because when all three bars close near their lows, an immediate decline tends to be quite strong.)

When all three bars close near their highs and a signal for a sustainable rally is given, the advance tends to be quite strong. Note that, no matter how strong this signal, if the trend is delayed (meaning it comes after the market has traded back through **am** MEJT) there is no indication as to the strength of the ensuing move. All that is needed in that case is that we go past the extreme hit after the am sequence completed. And that target need not fall by much.

The following patterns tend to lead to trends which are weak, even if they are sustainable:

- **Am+1 and am+2, considered together, include prices over and under am MEJT.**

The rule here is that the strongest trends are preceded by the strongest moves in the am sequence. When the market does not make up its mind where it is going during that sequence, the ensuing move tends to be weaker.

- **One of the am+1 or am+2 bars closes in its upper half and the other in its lower half.**

This is another sign of an indecisive move.

Unsustainable trends

It is important that the rules for unsustainable trends are understood.

- If **am+2** closes within the range of the **am** bar, there is no attempt to trend and any market move during the morning is unsustainable.

- If **am+2** does not go past the extreme of **am+1** during its attempt to trend, the attempt has failed and any market move during the morning is unsustainable.

- If **am+2 has a narrow range**, any market move during the morning is unsustainable.

- If **am+2 does not take out a significant level** (the prior close or the extreme of the first 35 minutes of trading) any market move during the morning is unsustainable.

- If **the criteria for sustainability are not met, then no move which starts before 10:45am CT will stick.** No matter how far prices go, S&P 500 should return to the reference bar, most likely within two trading days. Note that a large move is not precluded. The rules just say such a move will retrace.

Examples of trend indication in the am sequence

Before I go over a few examples, here is a checklist that you should keep in mind to help you focus on what we have covered already:

Checklist

1. Is there a valid signal or is there an unfilled gap?

2. What is the reference bar?

3. Is there an attempt to trend?

4. Is the attempt sustainable?

It pays to ask oneself a fifth question as well:

5. What is the target of the move? In general, sustainable moves tend to take out prior day's close or a swing high (or low).

Example 1

Figure 2.7 – 30 January 2009

- There was no unfilled gap, so the am signal counted.
- Am+2 had a lower low and lower high than **am+1**, so the market was attempting to decline.
- Am+2 was a long bar, closed near its low and its low undercut the prior day's close and the low of the first 35 minutes of trading. Therefore the trend was sustainable.

- Am MEJT was the reference bar.

The am prediction was for a further decline. There was resistance in the price range of the reference bar (**am MEJT**) and, so long as it was not violated, the signal was immediate and the decline was favoured to be strong.

Figure 2.8 – 30 January 2009 (II)

As you can see in Figure 2.8, MEJT accurately called for a sizeable drop and identified a resistance area for a midday rally.

Example 2

Figure 2.9 – 3 February 2009

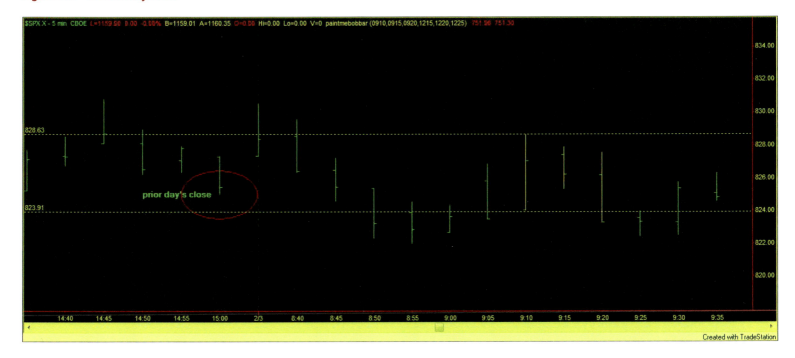

- There was a gap, but it filled before **am MEJT** printed, so an am signal was given.

- Am MEJT was the reference bar.

- Am+2 was a long bar, closed in its lower half and its low took out the significant level of the prior day's close. Therefore, the trend was sustainable. **Am+2** did not close far below **am** itself, so a sustainable trend was less likely to decline a lot.

As there was trading under **am+2** the minimum requirement was technically satisfied. However, we almost always get more; at the very least the undercutting of a swing low is expected – this is the target of the move. That initial (optional) target was the swing low of the first 35 minutes of trading (indicated by the white arrow in Figure 2.10).

Figure 2.10 – 3 February 2009 (II)

As there was trading over the reference bar before that target was hit, the trend became delayed. The new target became the swing low after the am sequence printed (indicated by the green arrow in Figure 2.10). Its preferred time for printing was within two trading days.

MEJT suggested that the rally on 3 February 2009, strong though it was, would reverse, most likely within two trading days, and targeted a return to the level indicated by the dotted green line in Figure 2.10. Note that while the S&P 500 will not necessarily stop declining when its MEJT target is hit, one should expect support just past the target price.

The prediction did not give an entry for a short position, but correctly said the rally would retrace and gave a reasonable price at which to exit from a short position.

Example 3

Figure 2.11 – 7 January 2009

- There was an unfilled gap, so there was no am signal.
- Am+1 had a higher high and lower low than **am** itself; it replaced it as the reference bar. Note that the reference bar still provided a resistance area. The reference bar high was 920.63; the subsequent high was 920.82. This is within our 0.20 tolerance.

- The fact that **am+2** had a lower range than **am+1** and gapped down has no significance because there was no am signal.
- The market tipped its hand by gapping down. There was resistance in the area of the reference bar.

Example 4

Figure 2.12 – 9 January 2009

- There was no unfilled gap, so there was an am signal.
- Am MEJT was the reference bar.
- Am+2 had a lower range than am+1, so the market attempted to decline.

The target was hit immediately. The market found support just under that level.

- Am+2 had a low which was under the significant level of the prior day's close. It was a long bar and closed in its lower half. Therefore a valid sell signal was given. The target was to undercut the swing low of the first 35 minutes of trading.

Figure 2.12 demonstrates that one should not enter a position just because a signal is given. For one thing, the trend could be delayed. For another, even if the trend is immediate one must consider the target and gauge whether the minimum profit forecast justifies taking an investment risk.

Those who were looking to enter the market on the long side conceivably could have used the entry given by the MEJT support level.

Example 5

Figure 2.13 – 12 January 2009

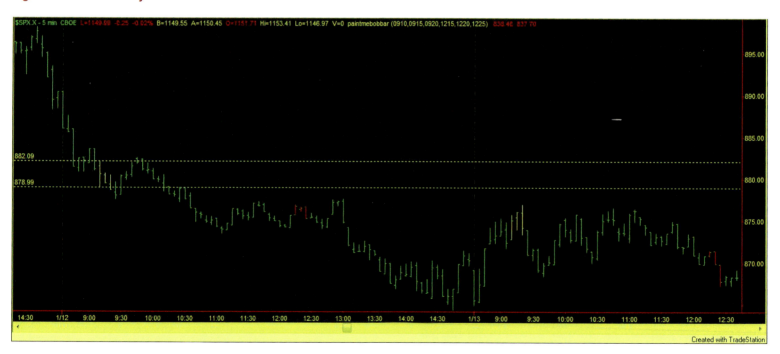

- The prior day's close was 890.35; the first bar's high showed as 890.40. However, the E-mini closed at 3pm CT the prior trading day at 886.75. The high print of the E-mini before **am MEJT** printed was 885.00. Therefore, there was an unfilled gap and there was no signal. It is important to remember to check futures and/or the SPDR S&P 500 ETF (ticker symbol SPY) to see whether or not there is an unfilled gap.

- Note that the resistance offered by the reference bar was violated by just over our 0.20 tolerance, but that violating this resistance does not constitute a buy signal.

The actions of the **am+1** and **am+2** bars had no predictive power on 12 January 2009 because the unfilled gap denied us an am signal.

Example 6

Figure 2.14 – 13 January 2009

- There was a gap, but it filled before **am MEJT** printed, so there was a signal.

- **Am MEJT** was the reference bar.

- **Am+1** closed near its high. **Am+2** closed near its low and within the **am MEJT** range. There was no attempt to trend.

- Because **am+1** and **am+2** did not attempt to trend, the odds were that the market would not attempt to trend either. All bars of the am sequence stayed within a narrow range and so did subsequent market action throughout the morning.

This pattern does not preclude a big move. However, it is less likely to occur without support from the am sequence and, if it does occur, is obligated to retrace into the range of the reference bar. Note that no move with staying power began before 10:45am (see Figure 2.15).

Figure 2.15 – 13 January 2009 (II)

Example 7

Figure 2.16 – 27 January 2009

- The market opened with a gap. It did not fill before **am MEJT** printed, but did fill during that bar. That is not good enough to satisfy the criterion. Since the gap did not fill in time, there was no am signal.

Note that the reference bar still provided support. People who were bullish, based on other factors, could have profited from using it as an entry point or stop loss area.

Example 8

Figure 2.17 – 9 February 2009

- There was no unfilled gap. There was a valid am signal and **am MEJT** was supported.
- **Am+2** had a higher high and higher low than **am+1**, so there was an attempted rally. **Am+2** was a long bar and closed in its upper half, but its high took out neither the prior day's close nor the high of the first 35 minutes of trading.

MEJT marked the day-long rally as unsustainable and forecast a return to the reference bar within two trading days.

Example 9

Figure 2.18 – 18 February 2009

- There was no unfilled gap, so there was an am signal.
- Am MEJT was the reference bar.
- Both **am+1** and **am+2** closed near their lows. However, **am+2** had a higher range than **am+1**. Therefore the attempt to decline was unsuccessful. There was no attempt to rally since **am+2** did not go over **am MEJT**.

- MEJT predicted the morning rally was unsustainable and forecast a return to the reference bar, usually within two trading days. Note that, not only did that happen, but that the reference bar provided support.

Example 10

Figure 2.19 – 12 March 2009

- There was no unfilled gap, so there was an am signal.

- **Am+2** had a higher range than **am+1**, so there was an attempt to trend. It was a long bar and closed in its upper half.

- The only issue remaining was whether or not a significant level was taken out. The level needs to be taken out by the high (not necessarily the close) of **am+2** if a sustainable advance is to be signalled. The first sustainable level was the prior day's close. **Am+2** took out that level, so a buy signal was generated and targeted the next significant level, the swing high near the close on 11 March 2009.

- **Am+2** did not take out the swing high near the close on 11 March 2009. Therefore the rally above it was marked as unsustainable. Had S&P 500 rallied after 10:45am, the move would have been sustainable.

This is an example of a failed target. S&P 500 did not follow the rules of the system and staged one of the greatest rallies in history without retracing to the reference bar. This failed target is, I believe, a postponed target. The rules say it should print at some time but offer no clue as to when. (Should that happen, the rules will have been followed after all.) While most of the time targets print within their preferred time frames, there are plenty of examples of failed targets occurring at or near the beginnings of giant moves. Bear this in mind if the target does not print in its preferred time frame.

3

The Am+3 Buy Signal

Before getting into this chapter, I should explain why I am writing about the am+3 buy signal at all.

When I began my medical practice one of the first things I did was to buy all the surgical instruments I thought I would ever need. There were a few tools I used on practically every case, and there were others I knew I would only use once in a blue, blue moon. But even though I hardly ever took these rarely-used tools out of the case, I knew that having them around made me better prepared to deal with an unusual situation.

It is for this same reason that I am writing about the **am+3** buy signal. This signal is one of those rare birds that can go a year or more between appearances, but when it occurs it is reliable and can generate significant profits.

The rules are pretty straightforward and all of them need to be present for the signal to trigger.

Rules for the am+3 buy signal

- **The am sequence gives a valid sell signal.**

Typically, but optionally, **am+1** and **am+2** are long bars, close near their lows and often undercut both the prior day's close and the low of the first 35 minutes of trading of the day on which the signal occurs.

- **The am+3 bar immediately begins a strong move up.**

Am+3 is the five-minute bar immediately following **am+2**; it begins at 9:20am CT. Often its low is noticeably above that of am+2, showing a rejection of its move down.

- **Without pausing to consolidate, S&P 500 surpasses the am MEJT high by more than 0.20.**

This completes the buy signal.

It should be noted that if there is a pause to consolidate, there is no signal; it is essential that the **am MEJT** high be overtaken with a forceful straight line move up. If one is not sure that the rally is strong enough to qualify, then assume it isn't.

- At this point there is a common, but optional, retracement into the **am MEJT** bar. Ideally S&P 500 should not close under **am MEJT** by more than 0.20.

- S&P 500 should then begin a strong rally, typically lasting into the afternoon and often into the final hour of the day, with few pullbacks.

This is a highly reliable signal. If one is not safely in the black when the afternoon begins, exit the trade.

Usually, but optionally, on the following day the rally is retraced and the **am+2** low is undercut. There is support in the first point under the **am+2** low, but that support is not obligated to hold.

It is worth mentioning that although the market usually likes symmetry, it makes an exception in this case – there is no corresponding **am+3** sell signal.

Examples of the am+3 bar buy signal

Example 1

The signal shown in Figure 3.1 is pretty much what we are looking for.

Figure 3.1 – 12 July 2005

In Figure 3.1 there was no unfilled gap, so there was an am signal. Am+2 had a lower high and lower low than **am+1** so there was an attempt to decline. Am+2 was a long bar, closed in its lower half and took out both the prior day's close and the low of the first 35 minutes of trading, giving a valid sell signal.

It would have been nicer if the low of **am+3** were noticeably higher than the close of **am+2**, but it will not always be the case that the signal will always fit every criterion perfectly. It also would have been nicer if the move over **am MEJT** was a bit quicker. However, note that the move came in a straight line and that there was no consolidation.

The pullback penetrated the **am MEJT** low, which is a bit deeper than usual, but at no point did it close below there. The rally was strong and lasted into the last hour of the day.

S&P 500 usually pulls back to undercut the **am+2** low the following day, but that did not happen here. This left a failed target (which was satisfied eventually).

Example 2

Figure 3.2 – 15 November 2005

There was no unfilled gap and **am+1** and **am+2** attempted to decline. Am+2 was a long bar, closed in its lower half and took out the prior day's close, giving a valid sell signal and targeting an undercutting of the low of the first 35 minutes of trading (so long as the S&P 500 did not trade past the reference bar, **am MEJT**).

Note the action of the **am+3** bar. It immediately took out the **am MEJT** high and gave us an **am+3** buy signal. The market rallied strongly with minimal pullbacks until the afternoon. The decline began sooner than one normally sees and, once it started, gave us a clue that something else was going on.

The am sequence sell signal remained active. Because the market traded over **am MEJT**, the trend that was forecast was delayed, but not denied. The market traded under the **am+2** low. Note that there was support there, but it did not hold as the market entered the last hour of trading.

Example 3

Figure 3.3 – 4 March 2003

The am sequence gave a sell signal and **am+3** began a rally.

S&P 500 traded higher than **am MEJT** but did not do so by over 0.20. There was no **am+3** buy signal and the am sequence sell signal remained in force. The target (which, as with all MEJT targets, is a minimum target and not necessarily a signal to stop and reverse) was to undercut the **am+2** low. Note that there was support in that area.

Example 4

Figure 3.4 – 14 May 2004

The set-up shown in Figure 3.4 offered the opportunity to make serious money.

There was no unfilled gap, so there was an am signal. **Am+1** and **am+2** attempted to decline, and the **am+2** bar went to the low of the day. (Note that because **am+1** and **am+2** collectively traded over and under **am** MEJT, S&P 500 was favoured to do so as well. That does not invalidate the sell signal.)

Am+3 immediately took out the **am** MEJT high and the **am+1** high as well. There was no consolidation at all. A brief pullback into the **am** bar gave a reasonable entry. The market rallied nearly to the last hour of the day.

The am sequence sell signal remained active. By the following morning it had been satisfied.

Example 5

Figure 3.5 – 12 June 2003

The gap filled before **am MEJT** printed, so the sell signal was valid. Note how the **am+3** low was higher than the **am+2** close, which is ideal.

This signal was profitable but did not deliver as much as one might have expected. The failure to deliver much by the time the afternoon started was a signal for investors on the long side to cash in their chips. The am sequence low did hold and a higher price was printed later on, but if the buy signal has not paid off by the time the afternoon starts it is best to exit the trade. Remember, there is an active am sequence sell signal in effect and just because the downtrend is delayed it does not mean the bears won't eventually win.

Example 6

Figure 3.6 – 20 July 2004

This set-up was better than the one shown in example 5. The **am MEJT**, **am+1** and **am+2** bars all went into free fall, each closing near its lows and with a gap to boot. The low of the day was taken out and everything appeared ready for the bears to enjoy a powerful decline.

After undercutting the **am+2** low briefly, which is unusual, **am+3** began a rally that lasted well into the last hour and the lone pullback of which did not quite make it to the **am MEJT** high.

Example 7

Figure 3.7 – 6 October 2005

The pattern shown in Figure 3.7 is worth studying as well. A valid sell signal was provided by the am sequence. **Am+1** closed near its high and **am+2** near its low, suggesting that, during the morning, a big move was less likely.

Despite the sell signal, **am+3** began a move which took out the **am MEJT** high. However, because of the consolidation before that happened, there was no **am+3** buy signal and the am sequence sell signal remained in effect. Lower prices were forecast, most likely within two days. This is what occurred.

Part 3

Afternoon Signals

4

Trading the MEJT Sequence

When I began day trading, I quickly came to the conclusion that afternoons were a pain. The market seemed to move around aimlessly and without conviction most of the time, as if it were waiting for the final hour of trading for something serious to begin. No one can make any money if he cannot predict where prices are going and I did not see a clear way to make sense of what went on between the time the lunch hour ended and the time the last hour began.

However, since I had some success with the am sequence, I decided to have another look at the patterns taking place in the afternoon. I wondered if big traders telegraphed their intentions after returning from lunch just as they did in the morning.

I found that not only were there three bars in the afternoon whose actions predicted future price action, but that the moves they predicted were more likely to fall within their preferred time frames. Afternoon action, it turned out, was more predictable than morning action. Furthermore, while the rules for trading the MEJT sequence in the afternoon were different to those for trading the am sequence in the morning, they were quite similar.

There are two differences between the rules for trading the morning and afternoon sequences that are worth emphasising:

1. It is common for a strong trend to begin in the morning. Much of the profit from trading the am sequence comes from jumping on board sustainable trends. It is far less common for a strong trend to begin in the afternoon. Consequently, much of the profit from trading the MEJT sequence[1] comes from fading trends which the rules say will not stick.

2. If S&P 500 is making a strong move (in either direction) in the morning, then after the am sequence completes the index should not trade through the am bar (with a 0.20 tolerance). If S&P 500 is making a strong move (in either direction) in the afternoon a slight penetration of the **MEJT** bar is allowed and is not unusual.

First, let's define the pm sequence.

---

[1]Remember that the MEJT sequence is the name given to the set of three bars that make up the afternoon signal.

Defining the pm sequence

- The **MEJT bar** (MEJT for short) is the five-minute bar beginning at 12:10pm CT.

- The **MEJT+1** bar is the next five-minute bar, beginning at 12:15pm CT.

- The **MEJT+2** bar is the subsequent five-minute bar, beginning at 12:20pm CT.

These three bars are known collectively as the MEJT sequence. The action of the MEJT sequence enables us to arrive at the MEJT prediction.

The satisfaction of the MEJT prediction often, but not always, takes place during the afternoon in which the sequence prints. Most of the time, the prediction is satisfied before the end of the next trading day (its preferred time).

There are a few terms one uses in describing the MEJT sequence which we did not employ during our discussion of the am MEJT sequence. These are:

- A *prior relative high* is a five-minute bar whose high is higher than the high of the bar to its immediate right and higher than the high of the bar to its immediate left. If either of these bars has a high at the same level, it is ignored and the bar to its immediate right or left is considered. It is not necessarily the high of a consolidation or price swing. A prior relative high occurs prior to the **MEJT** bar.

- A *prior relative low* is a five-minute bar whose low is lower than the low of the bar to its immediate right and lower than the low of the bar to its immediate left. If either of these bars has a low at the same level, it is ignored and the bar to its immediate right or left is considered. It is not necessarily the low of a consolidation or price swing. A prior relative low occurs prior to the **MEJT** bar.

- A *prior relative extreme* is either a prior relative low or a prior relative high.

- A *swing high or low* is a high or low of a market move, or swing.

Figure 4.1 – 16 November 2009

Basic principle behind the MEJT prediction

Most of one's profits from trading the MEJT prediction come from fading unsustainable trends. When an unsustainable trend is signalled, targets are created. It is these targets which help one to profit; one usually does not act on the signal immediately after it is given.

The basic principle behind the MEJT prediction is this:

> The **MEJT** bar is the standard reference bar. The actions of the **MEJT+1** bar and the **MEJT+2** bar determine whether or not the market will attempt to trend. The action of the **MEJT+2** bar determines whether or not the attempt will succeed.

In order for a trend to be sustainable, all the criteria for sustainability must be met. Otherwise, the trend is marked as unsustainable, and the market will return to or through the reference bar.

Let's go over the essentials of the pm sequence, the first listed of which are very similar to the rules for the am sequence.

MEJT is the default reference bar. The reference bar acts as a support/resistance level which can remain significant for days even after targets from the MEJT prediction have printed. If **MEJT+1** has a higher high and lower low than MEJT, it replaces it as the reference bar. If **MEJT+2** has a higher high and lower low than both **MEJT** and **MEJT+1** then it becomes the reference bar.

The action of the **MEJT+1** bar and the **MEJT+2** bar determines whether or not the market will attempt to trend. (In fact, the action of these two bars tends to mimic the subsequent action of the market itself.) One assesses the action of these two bars by looking at their high to low ranges, their closes and their ability to escape the ranges of the bars which preceded them.

For example, if **MEJT+2** has a higher high and higher low than **MEJT+1**, the market is attempting to rally. If **MEJT+2** has a lower high and lower low than **MEJT+1**, the market is attempting to decline. If both **MEJT+1** and **MEJT+2** are unable to break outside of the MEJT range, there is no attempt to trend and subsequent moves tend to have a narrow range. If **MEJT+2** closes within the MEJT range, there is no attempt to trend.

For a market to attempt to trend higher, **MEJT+2** must have a higher high than **MEJT+1**. It is not necessary for it to have a higher low. For a market to attempt to trend lower, **MEJT+2** must have a lower low than **MEJT+1**. It is not necessary for it to have a lower high.

The action of the **MEJT+2** bar determines whether or not any attempt to trend will be sustainable. Because of this one may consider it, and not MEJT itself, as the most important bar of the MEJT sequence. When a trend is strong and immediate, the **MEJT+2** bar certainly gives more information than either of the other two bars. Under this circumstance, **MEJT+1** gives the next most information. MEJT itself usually adds very little.

Before going into more of the rules, it is useful to restate the definitions of two more terms:

- An *immediate trend* is one which begins before the market passes through the reference bar. There is a 0.20 tolerance for this. For example, if S&P 500 is at 1000 and the MEJT prediction is for a rally, then an immediate trend is one which begins before the market prints a price under (not at) 999.80.

- A *delayed trend* is one which begins after the market passes through the reference bar.

Here are the rules for trading the MEJT sequence.

Rules for trading the MEJT sequence

In order for the three-bar MEJT sequence to signify a sustainable trend, **MEJT+2** must be a long bar, close in its distal (away from the **MEJT** bar itself) half and take out a prior relative extreme.

Long, as in *long bar*, is a relative term. A bar 0.30 in length is too small. A bar 0.50 in length is long enough. However, the longer the bar and the further away from MEJT the close, the better the ensuing trend if the trend is immediate. If the trend is delayed, the length of the bar and the distance of the close have no such predictive power.

Whether a move is immediate or delayed, the target of the move tends to print before the end of the next trading day (its preferred time). If the target does not print within its preferred time, it is defined as a failed target. It is my belief that failed targets are actually postponed targets; they print eventually, although there is no time limit in which they must do so. Specifically, if MEJT signals that a move is not sustainable, the market should return to the reference bar. If the market had an unmet obligation to trade past the reference bar, then trading there becomes the target.

When a sustainable trend occurs before the market trades through the reference bar, the strength of the **MEJT+1** and (to a greater extent) the **MEJT+2** bars tends to mimic the strength of the trend which was signalled. The longer these bars and the farther away from MEJT their closes, the more forceful the subsequent action of S&P 500 in the same direction.

Trends which are strong and immediate should be preceded by the appropriate MEJT prediction. The most bullish MEJT prediction would come if MEJT was a long bar which closed at its high, **MEJT+1** was a longer bar which closed at its high and **MEJT+2** was the longest bar of all and closed at its high as well. Ideally, there would be little overlap between the bars, but such ideal situations hardly ever happen. *The point to remember here is that a strong advance can ensue if these bars are rallying with enthusiasm.*

The most important move would be signalled by the **MEJT+2** bar, an important move would be signalled by the **MEJT+1** bar and little information would be added by the **MEJT** bar. (I cannot say no information would be added because when all three bars close near their highs, an immediate advance tends to be quite strong.) Note that, no matter how strong this signal, if the trend is delayed (meaning it comes after the market has traded back through MEJT with a 0.20 tolerance)

there is no signal as to the strength of the move. All that is needed in that case is that the market moves past the prior relative extreme hit after the MEJT sequence completed. There is support or resistance just beyond that level; accordingly it is common for that prior relative extreme to be penetrated only slightly.

Sustainability of patterns

The following patterns tend to lead to trends which are weak, even if they are sustainable:

- **MEJT+1** and **MEJT+2**, considered together, include prices over and under MEJT. The rule here is that the strongest trends are preceded by the strongest moves in the MEJT sequence. When the market does not make up its mind where it is going during that sequence, the ensuing move tends to be weaker.

- One of the **MEJT+1** or **MEJT+2** bars closes in its upper half and the other in its lower half. This is another sign of an indecisive move being on tap.

The rules for unsustainable trends in the MEJT sequence are similar, but subtly different, to those for the am sequence. Recall that if the am sequence says a move in the morning is unsustainable, then S&P 500 must retrace to the reference bar and trade there on or after 10:45am CT before a sustainable move can begin.

If the MEJT sequence says that a move in the afternoon is unsustainable then before a sustainable move can begin these criteria must be met:

- S&P 500 must trade over the reference bar,

- S&P 500 must trade under the reference bar,

- S&P 500 must trade within the reference bar on or after 1:25pm CT.

Circumstances where unsustainable trends are indicated are:

- If **MEJT+2** closes within the range of **MEJT** there is no attempt to trend and any attempt to trend before the above criteria are met is unsustainable.

- If **MEJT+2** does not go past the extreme of **MEJT+1** in the direction of its attempt to trend, the attempt has failed and any attempt to trend before the above criteria are met is unsustainable.

- If **MEJT+2** has a narrow range, any market move is unsustainable until the above criteria are satisfied.

- If **MEJT+2** does not take out a prior relative extreme (a high if S&P 500 is trying to rally or a low if S&P 500 is trying to decline) any move is unsustainable until the criteria are met.

If the criteria for sustainability are not met, then no move which starts before 1:25pm CT will stick. No matter how far prices go, S&P 500 should return to or through the reference bar, most likely before the end of the next trading day. Note that a large move is not precluded. The rules just say such a move will retrace. There is no leeway in this time requirement. If a move begins just seconds before 1:25pm prints, it should not stick.

There is some leeway on the price, however. If the rules require the market to print over and under MEJT before a trend becomes sustainable, then the earliest the price requirement can be met is the close of the **MEJT+2** bar (and not the open of the subsequent bar). In other words, if S&P 500 must trade over and under MEJT, and if **MEJT+2** closes over **MEJT**, then it need print no other price over **MEJT** to satisfy the criteria; the market just needs to trade under **MEJT**. Similarly, if **MEJT+2** closes under **MEJT**, prices need not print under there again to satisfy the requirement that the market must trade over and under the bar.

Once a few bars have passed since the completion of the MEJT sequence and once S&P 500 has traded beyond the range of the MEJT sequence, there is a 0.20 tolerance for meeting the requirement that S&P 500 trade through the other extreme of the reference bar in situations where that is called for by the rules. Even when this tolerance satisfies the requirement for trading through the reference bar, S&P 500 tends to trade through the bar anyway even though the target is no longer required.

Examples of trend indication in the pm sequence

Before looking at some examples, let's remind ourselves of the checklist we introduced in chapter two:

Checklist

1. What is the reference bar?

2. Is there an attempt to trend?

3. Is the attempt sustainable?

4. What is the target? (In general, one should overtake a prior relative extreme or make a tradable move in the direction signalled.)

Example 1

Figure 4.1 – 14 December 2005

- Figure 4.1 demonstrates the most common pattern seen in the afternoon. The three MEJT bars are shown in red. MEJT itself was the reference bar.
- MEJT+1 and MEJT+2 attempted to trend, in this case higher.
- MEJT+2 did not extend high enough to take out the prior relative high. Therefore the trend was unsustainable.
- The rules say the market will pull back to undercut the MEJT bar low and will be within the MEJT range on or after 1:25pm CT before a sustainable trend begins.

Figure 4.2 – 14 December 2005 (II)

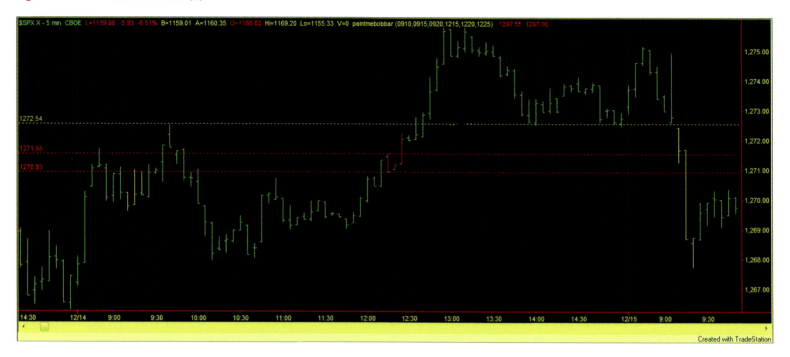

The prediction succeeded.

Example 2

Figure 4.3 – 13 December 2005

- In Figure 4.3 we see that both **MEJT+1** and **MEJT+2** were narrow bars which stayed completely within the range of MEJT. There was no attempt to trend.
- The rules say any trending attempt beginning before S&P 500 traded over and under the reference bar, and before 1:25pm has passed, should fail.
- This rally began too early; the rules say it should fail and prices return to the high of the reference bar, most likely before the end of the next trading day.

Figure 4.4 – 13 December 2005 (II)

The retracement did not occur during the next day of trading, so there was a failed target. Failed targets tend to print at some future time and this one printed the next morning.

Example 3

- In Figure 4.5 MEJT was the reference bar.

- MEJT+2 had a higher high than MEJT+1 and went past the MEJT high as well, so there was an attempt to trend higher.

- MEJT+2 had a range of 0.12. This is too short for the trending attempt to qualify as sustainable. If the range of MEJT+2 is 0.30 or smaller, the trending attempt did not succeed. A length over 0.50 points is large enough. If the range is between 0.31 and 0.50 points the signal is muddled. I do not have enough data to make a prediction because this situation has occurred very infrequently during the eight years I have been following the indicators.

- The rules call for S&P 500 to trade under MEJT and wait an hour before making a sustainable move. MEJT+2 closed over the range of MEJT, so it was not necessary for prices to trade there again.

Figure 4.6 – 23 December 2005 (II)

The prediction succeeded.

Example 4

Figure 4.7 – 27 December 2005

- MEJT+1 had a higher high and lower low than MEJT, so it replaced MEJT as the reference bar.

- MEJT+2 had a lower low than MEJT+1. Therefore the market attempted to trend lower.

- MEJT+2 was a long bar, closed in its lower half and took out the prior relative low; the attempt to decline was marked as sustainable.

- The rules called for lower prices to print. There were no nearby swing lows to act as targets. So long as the move was immediate (meaning the market did not trade over the reference bar) the required target was for the market to trade under MEJT+2 and the expectation was that the market would do so by a tradable amount (usually a couple of points or more). MEJT+1 and MEJT+2 collectively traded over and under MEJT and in these circumstances, more often than not, a modest decline should be expected, rather than an extensive one. Furthermore, the market tends to act in a similar fashion to the way these two bars act. When these two bars trade over and under MEJT, the market tends to do so as well.

Figure 4.8 – 27 December 2005

The market decline exceeded our minimum expectations although it took more than two full days for it to do so. As far as a day trader was concerned, taking a modest gain was justifiable.

Eventually the market traded higher than the **MEJT** high.

Example 5

Figure 4.9 – 30 December 2005 (II)

- MEJT was the reference bar.

- MEJT+1 and MEJT+2 attempted a decline.

- MEJT+2 was a long bar, closed in its lower half, and took out the prior relative low.

- The attempt to decline was sustainable and the prediction was for a further decline.

- S&P 500 immediately traded over the reference bar, so the decline was delayed. The ensuing rally was deemed unsustainable. The target for the subsequent decline was to undercut the swing low.

- The swing low was undercut by the next trading day, its preferred time. Note support in that area. A strong rally ensued.

Example 6

Figure 4.10 – 3 February 2006

- MEJT was the reference bar.
- MEJT+1 and MEJT+2 attempted to trend.
- MEJT+2 was a long bar and closed in its upper half. The MEJT sequence took out the prior relative high, which was the MEJT-2 bar. Note that it is not necessary for the MEJT+2 bar to overtake the prior relative high for the trending attempt to be sustainable. If any of the three bars overtake the prior relative high this will do.
- In these circumstances, the rules suggest there will be a rally. At a minimum S&P 500 should trade over the MEJT+2 high. If the trend were immediate, the strength of the MEJT+1 and MEJT+2 bars would favour a good rally.

Figure 4.11 – 3 February 2006 (II)

It can be seen in Figure 4.11 that the market immediately undercut **MEJT**.

The minimum target had already been met since the **MEJT+2** high had been exceeded.

The rules said any decline beginning before 1:25pm CT would not stick, but that prices would return to the **MEJT** bar. Note how that bar acted as resistance for hours.

These charts demonstrate that, no matter how promising a buy signal looks, one must recall that the buy signal merely means that a target at a higher price has been created. It alone does not give an entry point, and it does not mean to buy immediately.

The market was in the midst of a sizeable decline when this signal was given. The MEJT sequence signal was not enough to override that trend. However, if one were correctly bearish during this decline, the range of the **MEJT** bar provided a good resistance area. One could have justified taking a short position there and possibly waiting until 1:25pm CT to do so. (A sizeable decline beginning before that time was not precluded. The rules just state that, should a sizeable decline occur, prices would retrace to the reference bar.)

Example 7

Figure 4.12 – 8 February 2006

- MEJT was the reference bar.

- The MEJT sequence gave a sell signal during a time when the market was rallying.

- The market traded under MEJT+2, so the minimum requirement was met. Almost always, however, the market trades past this minimum required price.

● Once the market traded over the high of the reference bar, the target for our expectation for more on the downside was to undercut the swing low occurring after the MEJT sequence completed (indicated by the dotted blue line). The market did that, after which the rally resumed. The market traded within the range of the reference bar after 1:25pm CT, so there was no requirement for prices to retrace.

Figure 4.12 demonstrates that general market conditions should be considered when using the MEJT rules. The market was rallying and trend followers were looking for entry points to the long side. Even though there was a MEJT sequence sell signal, the rules gave one a reasonable target for a long entry based on both time and price.

The MEJT sequence favoured not taking a long position before 1:25pm printed and provided a support area at just the right price.

Example 8

Figure 4.13 – 15 February 2006

- MEJT was the reference bar.

- All three **MEJT** bars closed near their highs. If the sustainability criteria were met and the move were immediate, there was the potential for a strong rally.

- **MEJT+2** had a higher high than **MEJT+1** and was 0.47 in length. The length criterion muddled the signal somewhat, but the market was in rally mode. Even without knowing the MEJT rules, one could have justified taking a long position. The question here was whether or not one should wait for a retrace. And that depended upon whether or not **MEJT+2** took out a prior relative high.

- The **MEJT+2** bar took out a five-minute bar whose high was higher than the highs of the bars to its immediate right and immediate left. That met the criterion, so there was no requirement for S&P 500 to retrace to the reference bar.

The point to note here is that the prior relative high was not the swing high of the prior consolidation, which occurred six bars before the 1274.05 high. The swing high did not need to be overtaken by **MEJT+2** for a sustainable move to occur; overtaking the prior relative high was sufficient.

5

The MEJT+3 or MEJT+4 Buy or Sell Signal

There once was a girl who had a cute curl,
Right in the middle of her forehead,
When she was good, she was very, very good,
And when she was bad she was horrid.

The girl from that nursery rhyme could have been the **MEJT+3** or **MEJT+4** buy or sell signal.

This signal works far more often than it fails, but it fails more often than the other signals in this book. When it fails it can fail badly. I personally use it either to exit a trade I am in or to time a trade in the direction I was intending to go anyway.

The rules for this signal are as follows:

- The MEJT sequence signals that S&P 500 must trade outside the range of the reference bar.
- On either the **MEJT+3** or **MEJT+4** bar the market does trade outside that range. It then returns to the range of the reference bar before the **MEJT+4** bar ends and usually, but optionally, stays there awhile.

- That completes the signal. The call is that the next move of consequence (meaning two to three points or more) will be in the direction opposite that of the move outside the **MEJT** range.

Anthropomorphically speaking, it is as if the market knows it must trade under **MEJT** (for example) before it is allowed to stage a rally which sticks. The market proceeds to get that requirement out of the way and then a new movement – of either bullish or bearish nature – can begin.

Let's look at some real examples of this signal.

Examples of the MEJT+3 and MEJT+4 buy or sell signal

Example 1

Figure 5.1 – 19 April 2006

In Figure 5.1 you can see an **MEJT+3** buy signal.

- MEJT+2 closed within the range of **MEJT**, so there was no attempt to trend. S&P 500 was required to trade under **MEJT**, over **MEJT**, and wait an hour before a move could be regarded as sustainable.

- MEJT+3 traded just under **MEJT**, fulfilling one of the price requirements. **MEJT+4** then took us immediately higher than the **MEJT** low. The signal indicated that the next move of consequence would be higher.

- The market moved slightly lower than **MEJT**, but the next move of consequence was up. Since the move began before 1:25pm CT, it was doomed to retrace.

Example 2

Figure 5.2 – 19 December 2005

- MEJT+1 ranged over and under MEJT, so it became the reference bar. MEJT+2 closed within its range, so there was no attempt to trend. The rules required S&P 500 to trade over and under the reference bar and wait an hour before any move could stick.

- MEJT+3 took the market higher than the reference bar; then prices immediately retraced into the range of the bar.

Figure 5.3 – 19 December 2005 (II)

It can be seen in Figure 5.3 that the market did move lower. The MEJT+3 sell signal worked perfectly. So did the MEJT sequence requirement that the market retrace into the reference bar.

Example 3

Figure 5.4 – 28 March 2006

- MEJT+2 did not take the market past the MEJT+1 low, so the attempt to trend lower failed. The sequence rules are that the market must go higher than the reference bar and wait an hour before any trend will stick.
- MEJT+3 took prices higher than MEJT, the reference bar. Prices immediately fell back into the MEJT range. The market had immediately satisfied its duty as to price, so a MEJT+3 sell signal was in force. A slight move higher did not prevent the signal from being fulfilled.
- Since the drop began before 1:25pm, we would have expected it to retrace.

Example 4

Figure 5.5 – 21 March 2006

Figures 5.5 and 5.6 show a situation where the **MEJT+3** and **MEJT+4** signal failed. The three-bar MEJT sequence made no attempt to trend. **MEJT+3** went lower than of the reference bar and the market retraced into its range before **MEJT+4** was over. The rules called for the next move of consequence to be higher.

Figure 5.6 – 21 March 2006 (II)

As can be seen in Figure 5.6, the signal failed badly.

The MEJT+3 or MEJT+4 signal is not rare. It can work over and over again, then fail a number of times in a row. It works far more often than it fails, so bear that in mind if you plan to trade based on its predictions.

Part 4

Additional Information From MEJT

6

The Ultimate Signal – A Very Reliable Indicator

An ultimate signal is about as close to a sure thing as one gets in technical analysis. It is common – one can expect to see a signal several times each week – and it works. From the summer of 2005 through the spring of 2010 there are only two cases in which the prediction called for by the signal has not yet printed.

First, a definition of when an ultimate signal is given:

If any of the six bars of the am sequence or the MEJT sequence is a reversal bar, it gives an ultimate signal.

There are two types of reversal bars:

1. An *outside reversal bar* has a higher high and lower low than the bar which immediately precedes it and closes very near, or at, its high or its low. The subsequent bar cannot have a higher high and lower low than the outside reversal bar. If the subsequent bar undoes the reversal, by going past the high of a reversal down or under the low of a reversal up, the signal should not be trusted. If an outside reversal bar closes near its high, an ultimate buy signal is given. If it closes near its low, an ultimate sell signal is given.

2. An ultimate *buy signal variant* is a long bar which extends beyond the lows of the bars to its immediate right and left, then reverses and closes at or near its high. The bar subsequent to it does not undo it by undercutting its low. It is similar to a hammer in candlestick theory, except that the price of the open does not matter. An ultimate *sell signal variant* is a long bar which extends beyond the highs of the bars to its immediate right and left, then reverses and closes at or near its low. The bar subsequent to it does not undo it by overtaking its high. It is similar to a shooting star in candlestick theory, except that the price of the open does not matter.

Ultimate means eventual. When an ultimate buy signal is given, it means that ultimately the market will trade higher. When an ultimate sell signal is given, it means that ultimately the market will trade lower. An ultimate signal offers no prediction as to the direction of the next move. And, although one usually need not wait too long (meaning more than a few days) for the target to be hit, there is no time limit on the signal being fulfilled.

Now let's look at some examples of the signal in action.

Examples of the ultimate signal

Example 1

Figure 6.1 – 13 October 2008

On the price chart in Figure 6.1 there was an opening gap, so there was no am signal. However, **am+1** had a higher high and lower low than **am** and it closed near its high. Ultimate signals count whether or not an am signal is present. Therefore the call was that, ultimately, higher prices would print. They did.

Example 2

Example 6.2 – 3 October 2008

MEJT+2 had a higher high and lower low than MEJT and MEJT+1 considered together. It became the reference bar and gave an ultimate sell signal. In addition, it was a long bar, closed near its low and took out a prior relative low (the MEJT−2 bar). It is most unusual for am+2 or MEJT+2 to be an outside reversal bar and become the reference bar as well. On those rare occasions when it happens, you should look for a very big move.

Figure 6.3 – 3 October 2008 (II)

As can be seen in Figure 6.3, S&P 500 had slipped over 100 points by the next day. Normally when **MEJT+1** and **MEJT+2** considered together trade over and under **MEJT** the market does so as well. However, when **MEJT+2** acts as it did here, that tendency is far less likely to become reality.

Example 3

Figure 6.4 – 8 October 2008

MEJT+2 gave an ultimate sell signal variant. An ultimate signal does not necessarily predict the direction of the next move. In this case the market did drop quite a few points and undercut the low of the MEJT sequence, so one could argue it had fallen enough. However, the market did not take out a swing low, which almost always happens. Ultimately it did.

An ultimate signal has a minimum target of 0.26 points (which is *extremely rare*). A typical target is two to three points or more, going past a swing extreme and going past the range of the three-bar sequence in which it occurs.

Example 4

Figure 6.5 – 10 October 2008

MEJT+2 gave an ultimate buy signal.

Figure 6.6 – 10 October 2008 (II)

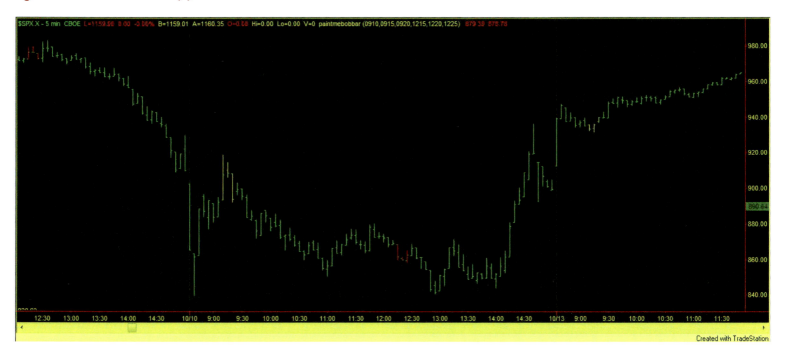

It can be seen in Figure 6.6 that the next move was down but, ultimately, the market traded up.

Example 5

Figure 6.7 – 12 March 2003

Figure 6.7 shows the bottom of the 2000-2003 bear market.

Am+2 gave an ultimate buy signal and was an outside reversal bar. It signalled a big move was coming, although not necessarily immediately. Do not ignore a signal like this one.

The MEJT sequence said no move beginning before 1:25pm would stick. It didn't, but it was over five years before that call was validated.

7

Targets – Required and Optional

Setting price targets is one of the most important parts of the MEJT system.

When MEJT gives a buy (or sell) signal, it is not an invitation to act immediately. It means that a price target has been set at a higher (or lower) price. It is important to have criteria for determining what the minimum potential gain is from acting on the signal for two reasons:

1. The risk/reward ratio must justify taking the trade.

2. Resistance is to be expected just past a target at a higher price, and support is to be expected just past a target at a lower price. Unlike targets in other systems, the price of S&P 500 typically goes past MEJT targets.

Different types of targets

There are different types of targets:

A *required target* is one which has to print, according to the rules of the system.

An *optional target* is one which almost always prints but which does not have to. For example, if a given price is targeted the target is satisfied if we come within 0.20 points

of that price. Although the target is no longer required to print, it usually does so anyway, making it optional.

Targets from unsustainable moves

If the am sequence signals a move is unsustainable then a return to the reference bar is required, with a 0.20 tolerance. If, for example, the market stages an unsustainable rally and the top of the reference bar for the am sequence is 1100.00, then 1100 is a required target. Once 1100.20 prints, the requirement has been met. The 1100.00 price becomes an optional target and it usually prints anyway.

If the MEJT sequence signals a move is unsustainable then it is required that prices trade over and under the reference bar before a sustainable move occurs. The first price eligible to meet the criterion is the close of **MEJT+2**. There is no 0.20 tolerance at this point; prices must trade outside the range of the reference bar. Once a price prints outside the reference bar and some time has passed (usually half an hour is enough) then there is a 0.20 tolerance for trading past the reference bar in the other direction.

For example, suppose **MEJT** is the reference bar and its range is 1100.00-1102.00. If the close of **MEJT+2** lies inside this range then 1100- (meaning 1099.99 but written this way by convention because 1100 is the **MEJT** low) and 1102+ (meaning 1102.01) are required targets with no tolerance. If 1099.99 prints (for example) then one of the price requirements has been met. The 1102+ price becomes a *required target* with a 0.20 tolerance.

It should not be trusted that the target has been satisfied by the 0.20 tolerance if prices have not moved out of a consolidation within the range of the reference bar. If one is using the 0.20 tolerance it is ideal for some time to pass as well (again, half an hour is usually enough). If, for example, the market were to drop to 1098 then 1102+ would become a required target with a 0.20 tolerance. Once 1101.81 printed, 1102+ would become an optional target.

Targets from sustainable moves

If one of the sequences signals a sustainable move, then a price print in the indicated direction is required.

If the move is immediate it must be far enough to indicate the signal has been validated. A move past a prior swing extreme is always high enough, no matter how small it is. There is a 0.20 tolerance for this.

For example, if the MEJT sequence says a move higher is sustainable and if **MEJT+2** closes at 1100.00, then any move over the prior swing high satisfies the call.

If the prior swing high was 1102.00 the required target for an immediate move is 1102.01 with a 0.20 tolerance. Once 1101.81 prints, the requirement has been met, and 1102.01 becomes an optional target.

If the prior swing high was 1101.00, then once 1100.81 printed 1101.01 would become an optional target. The significance of the target is that, even if the move were to be immediate, the minimum gain here would be very little. It would be more beneficial if the move higher were delayed because the potential gain would be much greater.

An extreme case, which is rare but which has occurred, would be if the prior swing high were 1100.01. The target would be 1100.01+ with a 0.20 tolerance, meaning 1099.81. Since MEJT+2 closed at 1100.00 the target would already have been met. One would know that a decline beginning before 1:25pm CT would not be sustainable, and one would have an optional target of 1100.01+, but there would be a significant likelihood that the signal would not give any tradable information.

Targets from situations where there is no swing extreme nearby

There are cases in which no swing extreme is nearby to give a target. A target should then be set based on price movement alone.

If the move is immediate and no swing extreme is taken out, that move must be significant to be sure the target has been met. A move of a point or two is always significant if there is no swing extreme which has printed recently. In cases of a fractional rally (for example) which does not take out a nearby swing extreme, one should make a note of the swing high made by the S&P 500 after the am sequence or MEJT sequence prints. Once the S&P 500 trades under the reference bar, that price (with a 0.20 tolerance) becomes an optional target.

A sustainable move almost always takes out a swing extreme if one has printed recently. If a move does not do so, then the price of the swing extreme printing after the am sequence or MEJT sequence becomes an optional target (with a 0.20 tolerance).

Targets from consolidations

Moves, especially unsustainable ones, have a tendency to end just past the prior consolidation closest in terms of price (not necessarily the consolidation nearest in terms of time) to the reference bar. The two qualifiers here are that one bar spikes outside the consolidation should be ignored and that (with that qualifier) there should be no price intersection within the range of the reference bar. On some occasions, the consolidation which does not intersect the three bar sequence provides a better guideline. This is a guideline only; it does not provide an optional target.

Targets from ultimate signals

An ultimate buy signal or ultimate sell signal must have a move of at least 0.26 in the signalled direction; this is a required target and taking out a swing extreme alone is not enough. By convention, this target is written as a price with ++ or − after it. A move as small as that is quite rare. Usually one gets at least two to three points (if the move is immediate) and the extreme of the sequence in which it occurs is taken out. If that does not happen, then once S&P 500 trades through the reference bar, the extreme of the swing after the signal was given becomes an optional target. The extreme of the sequence in which it occurs becomes an optional target as well.

Some special things to watch out for are:

1. One should expect resistance over a higher priced target and support under a lower priced target. The resistance is greatest in the first point past the target, significant in the second point past the target, present in the third point past the target and absent once prices move over three points past the target.

2. If prices reverse within 0.20 of a target (defined as a direct hit) then a reversal of eight to ten points, while not required, is common. The move is not required to go to completion, but if an eight to ten point move happens, many times it will stop right there.

Signals from failed targets

There are also two important signals from failed targets:

If two previous failed targets in the same direction print in the same day, one should expect a good move (usually at least ten points) in the other direction before the end of the next day. This applies only if the targets are failed (meaning they did not print in their preferred time frames) and only if two and only two targets print. As a further condition, I require that the two failed targets come from different days, although I am not certain that this is necessary; I just don't have enough evidence to state otherwise. For example:

- If the S&P 500 rallies past two (and only two) failed targets in the same day, look for a decline of ten or more points before the following day's close.

- If the S&P 500 declines past two (and only two) failed targets in the same day, look for a rally of ten or more points before the following day's close.

Multiple failed targets all under or all over current prices and occurring within a narrow period of time are often indicative either of a major change in trend or of a strong continuation of the present trend. Use this information as a sign that market momentum is changing. This signal was present right after the market top in October 2007.

- There remain failed targets from 11 October 2007, 15 October 2007 and 1 November 2007. This cluster is a sign of a market top.

- There remain failed targets from 2 September 2008, 9 September 2008 and 22 September 2008. This cluster is a sign of a strongly trending market.

I have not seen clusters like these last very long during periods of market consolidation.

A few examples should suffice to convince you that setting targets increases the value of the MEJT system.

Examples of setting targets

Example 1

Figure 7.1 – 16-22 March 2010

The yellow and red horizontal lines in Figure 7.1 show the ranges of the reference bars for 19 January 2010 (the penultimate day on the chart, with vertical white lines separating the days).

Am+2 gave an ultimate buy signal and prices immediately dropped. The high of **am+2** was 1163.05; however there was an intraday gap since the low of **am+1** was 1163.29. That meant the high of the bar's true range was 1163.29. Adding 0.26 gave a required target of 1163.55 (with no 0.20 tolerance). This can be written as a target of 1163.29++. There were optional targets of exceeding the high of the three+ bar am sequence (1164.46 with a 0.20 tolerance) and rallying two to three points (1165.55-1166.55). This latter target was cancelled since the move higher was not immediate. Often a prior swing high is taken out as well (point 1 at 1166.47.)

Since **am+2** did not close in its lower half, the decline was unsustainable and another required target of returning to the reference bar low (1163.56) was established.

Common places to look for the unsustainable decline to end were just under the prior consolidation which did not overlap the reference bar (white box on 18 March) and just under the prior consolidation which did not overlap the am sequence (white box on 16 March).

Note how well the targets worked:

- The first drop on 19 March bottomed within two points of the consolidation of 18 March.

- The drop of 22 March bottomed within one point of the consolidation of 16 March.

- The reference bar on 19 March had a range of 1163.56-1164.46. The high at white point 2 was 1164.92. Resistance was present.

- The swing high at white point 3 was 1167.05, within one point of the high at white point 1. Resistance was present again.

- The MEJT sequence established required targets over and under the reference bar. Both were met easily.

Example 2

Figure 7.2 – 23 March 2010

In the price chart shown in Figure 7.2, **am MEJT** gave an ultimate buy signal. Its high was 1167.40. That gave a required target of 1167.40++, or 1167.66 (add 0.26), and optional targets of 1169.66-1170.66 (add two to three points) so long as the low of the reference bar was not undercut, and 1168.79+ (take out the high of the am sequence).

Am+2 was a long bar, closed in its upper half and took out the swing high of the prior day as well as the high of the first 35 minutes of trading. Therefore a rally was sustainable. Note that, since **am+1** closed in its lower half, the odds were against a strong rally occurring during the morning.

The high at point 1 was 1169.42; the question then became whether that was enough to satisfy the buy signals. It was a rally of 0.63 points, so the market did not really have to go any higher. However, the am sequence buy signal usually generates a gain of at least a point or two; traders should be on the alert for more than just a 0.63 advance. Once prices traded under the reference bar the swing high at point 1 became an optional target and the two to three point rally optional target from the ultimate buy signal was cancelled.

The high at point 2 was 1169.59. That satisfied the remaining optional target. As the market reversed within 0.20 of the target (a direct hit) a strong drop was possible, but not required.

The MEJT sequence had given a valid buy signal. Once prices surpassed the swing high at point 1 there was no requirement to go any farther. However, normally a MEJT buy signal is good for at least one or two points. Since this did not occur, point 2 became an optional target once the market undercut the reference bar. The optional target was satisfied at point 3.

The ensuing rally was not required to retrace even though it began before 1:25pm CT because the MEJT sequence indicated a rally would be sustainable. However, it retraced anyway. Note that there was support at the range of the **am MEJT** bar on both 23 March and 24 March.

Example 3

Figure 7.3 – 17 January 2007

In Figure 7.3, **am+2** closed within the **am** MEJT range. Therefore there was no attempt to trend. Once the market rallied before 10:45am CT there was a required target of a return to the range of the **am** bar.

Am+1 gave an ultimate sell signal. That gave us a required target of dropping 0.26 (1430.53–), an optional target of taking out the swing low at point 1 and an optional target of dropping two to three points if the move was immediate. The drop to point two satisfied all but the last target. Once the market traded over the reference bar the two to three point drop was cancelled as an optional target. Note that there was support under that level anyway at point 3.

MEJT+2 did not extend past **MEJT+1**, so any attempt to trend before 1:25pm CT was unsustainable. One common place for the unsustainable rally to end is just past the prior consolidation (white rectangle). Point 4 shows that the consolidation stopped there.

The afternoon drop began too soon. A return to the low of the reference bar was targeted. Note that there was resistance when the market satisfied the target at point 5.

Example 4

Figure 7.4 – 18 January 2007

In Figure 7.4, **am+2** gave an ultimate buy signal. That gave a required target of rallying 0.26 from its high, an optional target of rallying over the high of the am sequence and an optional target of rallying two to three points if the move was immediate. The swing high at point 1 met all of these targets.

MEJT gave an ultimate sell signal. It was satisfied before the end of the day.

MEJT+2 gave an ultimate buy signal. That gave a required target of rallying 0.26, a required target of trading over the reference bar (with a 0.20 tolerance), and an optional target of rallying two to three points if the market rallied immediately.

The reference bar high was 1429.30. S&P 500 rallied to 1429.39. This was within 0.20 of the target for a direct hit and a quick drop ensued, although it stopped short of its usual (but not required) maximum of eight to ten points.

The drop began before 1:25pm so there was a required target of returning to the low of the reference bar, which was satisfied the next day.

Note that when a sequence gives both ultimate buy and ultimate sell signals one expects each of them to be satisfied. Note also that **MEJT+1** closed at its low and **MEJT+2** near its high. This is not a common precursor to a sustainable move. A trader should be on the lookout for a quick scalp profit and a retracement.

Example 5

Figure 7.5 – 30 March 2010

In Figure 7.5, **MEJT** gave a valid sell signal. **MEJT+2** was a long bar, closed in its lower half and took out the prior relative low at point 1.

The next target was to undercut the swing low at point 2. **MEJT+2** had done that, so there was no need to go any lower.

However, S&P 500 almost always gives us more when a **MEJT** sell signal is generated. Once prices traded over the **MEJT** high, there was an optional target of undercutting the swing low at point 3. That happened the next day, on 31 March.

8

Support – Overt and Covert

The ranges of the **am MEJT** and **MEJT** bars can act as support or resistance areas for days after the bars print. This is true even if an unfilled gap denies us an am signal. This is known as *overt support* or *overt resistance.*

On days in which the **am MEJT** and **MEJT** sequences are far apart and without overlap one can often find support or resistance at Fibonacci targets which can be generated from these bars. This is known as *covert support* or *covert resistance.*

In order to find these covert levels, one needs to create a Fibonacci grid. In TradeStation you can do that by going to the drawing menu and, under Fibonacci Tools, choose **<Price Retracement Lines>**. Dragging the mouse across the screen will create a Fibonacci grid. Right clicking will allow you to choose the 23.6%, 38.2% and 61.8% retracement levels.

Then, use the 0% and 23.6% lines to measure the distance between the 38.2% and 61.8% lines on the grid. Arrange those two lines so they touch the outermost edges of the **am** and **MEJT** bars. Hidden support and resistance areas frequently appear at the 0% or 100% lines. See Figure 8.1 for an illustration of this.

Figure 8.1 – a Fibonacci grid drawn in TradeStation to indicate covert support and resistance lines 19 March 2007

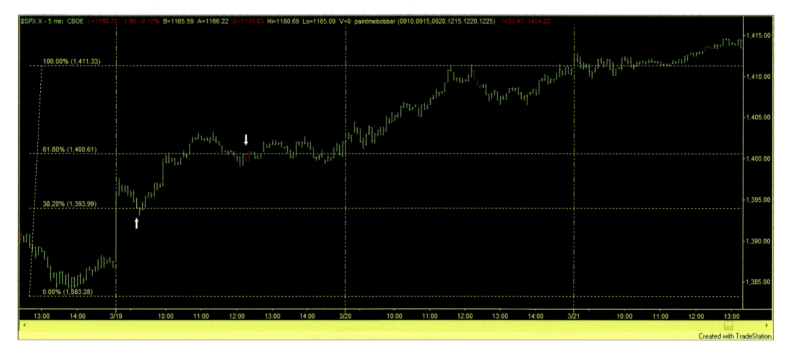

At times the effort produces no useful information, but at other times the lines pick up significant levels even a week into the future. The upper and lower lines are 261.8% extensions of the range between **am** and **MEJT**. Less frequently, other Fibonacci extensions can work. Taking Figures 8.2 and 8.3 together you can see the power of the Fibonacci grid to reveal – in this case – a future resistance level.

Figure 8.2 – a further Fibonacci grid drawn onto a price chart 20 March 2007

Figure 8.3 – the Fibonacci grid indicates a future resistance level 20 March 2007 and subsequent days

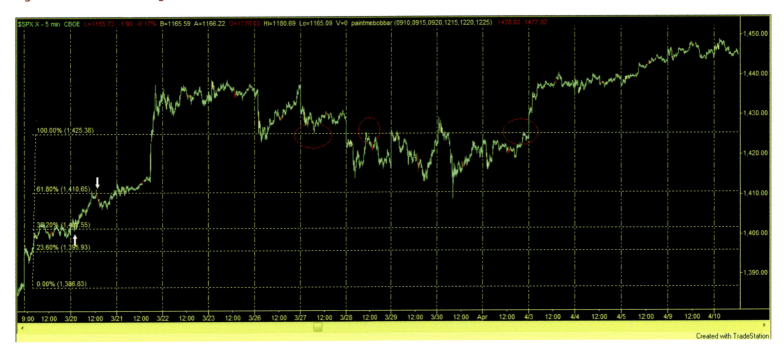

Another trick is to use what I call a MEJT grid. Make a Fibonacci grid with values of 9, 14.6, 23.6, 38.2, 50 and 61.8%. On a day in which the sequences do not overlap (and ideally when they are far apart) try setting each of these levels so that one of them and the 0% line touch the outermost extremes of the **am** and **MEJT** bars (as shown in Figure 8.4).

Figure 8.4 – the 0% and 61.8% Fibonacci levels touching the outermost extremes of the am and MEJT bars 6 May 2008

Now slide the grid so that either the 0% or 100% level touches the innermost extreme of the **MEJT** bar (as shown in Figure 8.5).

Figure 8.5 – the Fibonacci grid adjusted so that the 0% level touches the innermost extreme of the MEJT bar 6 May 2008

For the next two or three days one can often find support and resistance at many of the lines on the grid (as shown in Figure 8.6).

Figure 8.6 – the Fibonacci grid indicates future support and resistance levels 6 May 2008 and subsequent days

This exercise can be fun in retrospect but, unfortunately, I have not been helped too much in using it to make predictions. I have found no way to tell in advance which Fibonacci level one should use to get the targets.

Let's look at a third example, just to provide further evidence of this phenomenon.

Figure 8.7 – the 0% and 23.6% Fibonacci levels touching the outermost extremes of the am and MEJT bars 7 May 2008

Figure 8.8 – the Fibonacci grid adjusted so that the 0% level touches the innermost extreme of the MEJT bar 7 May 2008

Figure 8.9 – the Fibonacci grid indicates a future support level 7 May 2008 and subsequent days

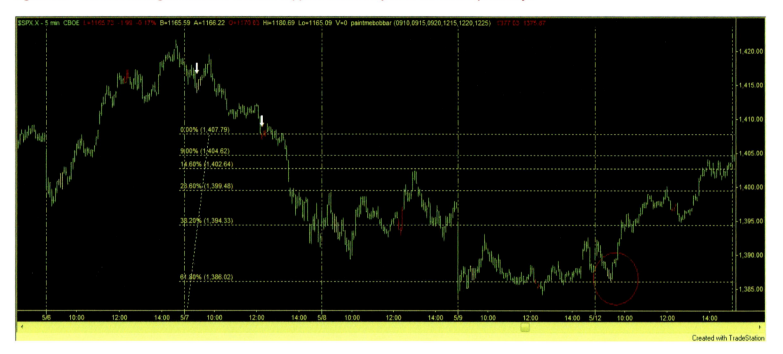

Part Five

The MEJT System In Practice

9

Putting the System to the Test

Introduction

For the benefit of anyone who likes to skip ahead to the final chapter to see how the system works before reading its rules, I will now repeat the conventions I use in this book.

- The times in all illustrations are Central Time (CT).

- The bars in yellow represent the three bars of the am MEJT sequence: **am**, **am+1** and **am+2**.

- The bars in red represent the three bars of the MEJT sequence: **MEJT**, **MEJT+1** and **MEJT+2**.

While using the figures in the book as you read through will be useful, I also recommend using TradeStation to pull up the charts on your computer. Using TradeStation, one can right-click on the price bars, go to the **<settings>** menu and change the date to bring up the same chart with greater clarity. One will also be able to identify specific prices.

In this chapter, I will go through a series of days of price data and show how the rules of the MEJT system are applied. I will explain what each rule says and review how its prediction fared. People who skipped ahead to this chapter should eventually pick up what the rules are. Those who believe they have learned the rules can test themselves by comparing their predictions with the ones given.

The examples contain over three weeks of trading with no days omitted. They include days when the market was in rally mode as well as its January 2010 peak and subsequent decline. They include days before and after holidays. The examples should convince you that the system, while not perfect, is reliable enough to use in trading. It gives at least one tradable call almost every day.

Please note that not every call in these examples worked and that not every call was tradable. When properly used, the system should improve one's trading results. Use it in addition to, rather than in place of, other forms of technical analysis.

Trading examples

Day 1

Figure 9.1 – 29 December 2009

The opening gap had not closed before the **am MEJT** bar (the first bar in yellow) printed. Therefore there was no signal. However, **am** itself gave an ultimate buy signal because it was a long reversal bar, closing near its high after making a low under that of both its neighbouring bars.

The signal says that, ultimately, S&P 500 should trade higher, ideally surpassing the high of the three bar **am MEJT** sequence.

MEJT+1 (the second bar in red) had a higher high and lower low than did MEJT and closed near its low, so it gave an ultimate signal. Since this reversal bar closed near its low, it predicted that, ultimately, lower prices would print. When **MEJT+1** has a higher high and lower low than **MEJT** it replaces it as the reference bar. MEJT+2 closed within the reference bar, so S&P 500 made no attempt to trend during the sequence.

The signal says that, ultimately, lower prices should print. It also says that no move beginning before S&P 500 has traded over and under the reference bar (MEJT+1 in this case) and that begins before 1:25pm CT will stick.

Result

All the predictions were satisfied. The prediction from the **am MEJT** sequence was not tradable because it did not predict the next move. The prediction from the MEJT sequence said the afternoon rally was doomed to failure; it had the potential to yield a big profit. Note how the reference bars from the morning and afternoon patterns provided support and resistance.

Day 2

Figure 9.2 – 30 December 2009

- There was an opening gap but it filled; therefore the **am MEJT** signal counted.

- **Am MEJT** was a reversal bar and closed near its low, giving an ultimate sell signal.

- **Am+1** closed near its low; **am+2** near its high.

- Thus the market attempted to decline from the reference bar, but the decline was not supported by the action of the **am+2** bar; it was not sustainable.

The signal said that, ultimately, lower prices would print. In addition, it said a move in the morning, not being supported by action of the **am MEJT** sequence, should reverse at least into the range of the **am MEJT** bar (dotted yellow lines). No move beginning before 10:45am CT should stick.

MEJT+1 and MEJT+2 both traded completely within the range of the **MEJT** bar (first red bar). This pattern often leads to very little movement over the next hour. But regardless of whether the market does a lot or a little during that hour, the fact remains that S&P 500 made no attempt to trend during the MEJT sequence. No move should stick until 1:25pm CT passes and S&P 500 trades on both sides of **MEJT**.

Result

The predictions all were satisfied. It would have been difficult to profit from the morning decline because ultimate signals do not tell us the next move. The am sequence did predict that the morning decline would not stick, which should have rewarded those who took the signal. The afternoon pattern yielded little but did warn traders that the decline right after the MEJT sequence completed was not sustainable.

Day 3

Figure 9.3 – 31 December 2009

- There was a gap, but it filled, so the **am MEJT** sequence gave a signal.

- **Am+1** had a higher high and lower low than the **am MEJT** bar, so it replaced it as the reference bar.

- **Am+2** closed within the range of **am+1**, so there was no attempt to trend.

The sequence predicted that, ultimately, lower prices would print. It also suggested that any move beginning before 10:45am CT would not stick.

MEJT+1 closed near its low; **MEJT+2** closed near its high and within the range of the **MEJT** bar. Thus there was no attempt to trend. Any move beginning before 1:25pm CT passed, and before S&P 500 traded over and under MEJT, was destined to retrace into **MEJT**.

Result

All the signals were satisfied. The big payoff came from fading (going against the prevailing market action) the late sell off, which the rules said would not stick. A retracement at least into the range of the morning reference bar (dotted yellow lines) was suggested by the morning pattern.

Day 4

Figure 9.4 – 4 January 2010

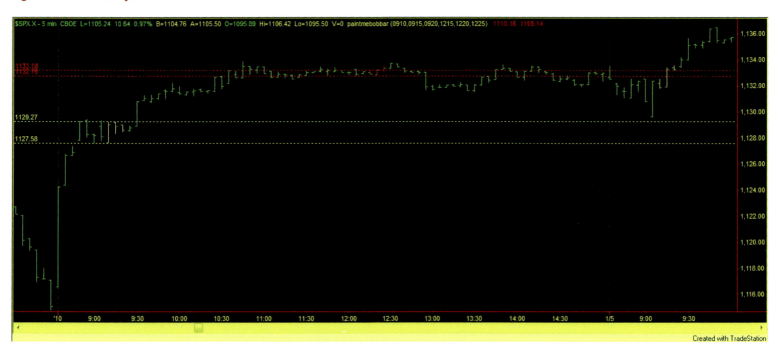

- There was an unfilled gap at the opening, so there was no **am** MEJT signal provided.

- **MEJT+1** had a higher high and lower low than MEJT, so it replaced it as the reference bar.

- **MEJT+2** had a higher range than **MEJT+1** and took out a prior swing high. (The **MEJT+2** high was 1133.45; the prior swing high was 1133.44.)

This allowed for a sustainable rally, which would be expected to overtake a prior swing high. That high was 1133.87 when the signal was given but, because the market traded under the reference bar (here **MEJT+1**) before taking out the target, the signal was delayed. The new swing high became 1133.73, which was the swing high made after the signal was given.

Result

All the predictions were fulfilled. There was no signal in the morning. The afternoon signal was not tradable because the minimum target was too close. It is possible that one could have gone long the following day, during which the signal was satisfied within its preferred time frame.

Day 5

Figure 9.5 – 5 January 2010

- The first bar of the day traded over the prior day's close.

- The day's second bar gapped down. That does not qualify as an unfilled opening gap, so the am signal counted.

- **Am+2** had a higher range than **am+1**, so the market attempted to rally.

Am+2 closed in its lower half, so the system predicted the rally would not succeed, but that prices would return at least to the high of the **am MEJT** bar (upper yellow line). Am+2 gave an ultimate sell signal, indicating that ultimately prices would trade lower, ideally taking out the low of the three bar am sequence (lower yellow line).

MEJT+2 had a lower range than **MEJT+1**, was a long bar, closed near its low and took out a prior swing low. The system predicted the market would trade lower, ideally before the next day's close. Typically a prior swing low would be undercut.

Results

The am signals were fulfilled. Traders could have profited by fading the morning rally, which the rules said should not be sustainable. Prices did trade lower after the MEJT signal, but did not take out the prior swing low of 1129.66. Note that **MEJT+1** was not a long bar which closed in its lower half. Without support from each of the last two bars of the sequence, the move is less likely to be strong in the predicted direction. Undercutting a swing low became an optional target.

On 20 January 2010 (over two weeks later) the market bottomed at 1129.25. This was in the ideal support area under the original target (1129.66-). However, since the market had traded over the **MEJT** high, the new target was to undercut the swing low at 1130.41. The 1129.25 swing low of 20 January was still within a support area identified by the MEJT rules.

Day 6

Figure 9.6 – 6 January 2010

- **Am+2** had a higher high and higher low than **am+1**, was a long bar, closed in its upper half and took out the prior day's high. The am sequence called for higher prices. Since **am+1** closed near its low, the outlook was that the advance was less likely to be strong. Once the **am** bar low was undercut, the target for the rally was to overtake the newly created prior swing high.

- **MEJT+2** did not have a higher range than **MEJT+1** and did not take out a prior swing high. The rules state that prices must to trade on both sides of **MEJT** and wait an hour before a sustainable move would begin. **MEJT+1** was a reversal bar signalling that, ultimately, lower prices would print.

Result

All the signals worked perfectly. The morning rally was unspectacular, although a prior swing high was overtaken. The market went nowhere before an hour passed, then dropped the following day. Traders following the system could have profited by buying the morning dip and by selling the afternoon rally.

Day 7

Figure 9.7 – 7 January 2010

- The morning's gap had not filled before the **am MEJT** bar printed, depriving us of a signal.

- **MEJT+2** did not overtake the **MEJT+1** high nor exceed a prior swing high. That meant no sustainable move would begin until an hour had passed and prices had undercut **MEJT**.

Note that **MEJT+2** closed over the **MEJT** high. Had the next bar (**MEJT+3**) begun a sizeable drop without trading over **MEJT**, traders following the system should have been on the alert for a return to the **MEJT** low and not for a price over the **MEJT** high.

Result

As predicted, the afternoon rally did not stick. Traders who faded it according to the rules would have been able to take their gains the following morning. Note support just under the **MEJT** low.

Day 8

Figure 9.8 – 8 January 2010

- **Am+1** had a higher high and lower low than **am**, replacing it as the reference bar. It gave an ultimate sell signal, which (ultimately) was vindicated.

- The unfilled gap meant there was no am signal.

- **MEJT+1** had was a bearish engulfing bar. It replaced **MEJT** as the reference bar and gave an ultimate sell signal.

- **MEJT+2** was a reversal bar, giving an ultimate buy signal. Its close within the **MEJT** range indicated that no move beginning before an hour passed, and before the market traded over and under **MEJT**, would stick.

The ultimate sell signal and ultimate buy signal in the same sequence also called for prices to trade over and under **MEJT**. When ultimate buy and ultimate sell signals are given in the same three-bar sequence the order in which they appear is usually the same as the order in which the market trades over and under **MEJT**. However, this pattern is not consistent enough to justify risking any money on. It did not work here.

Result

The market traded under **am+1** by enough to satisfy the sell signal. However, prices neither dropped by a few points nor undercut a prior swing low. The market having traded over the reference bar, the optional target of undercutting the subsequent swing low, targeting 1138.69-, was left; this was satisfied later in the month. As for the afternoon, the market undercut a swing low and waited past 1:25pm to begin its rally. **MEJT**'s job was done.

On 21 January 2010 there was a target of 1138.89 that did not fill in its preferred time frame. This is almost the same number as the 8 January target and that is no accident. **MEJT** bars tend to be significant even after their targets print.

Day 9

Figure 9.9 – 11 January 2010

- The unfilled gap deprived us of an am signal.

- The **am+2** ultimate buy signal still counted, telling us that, ultimately, higher prices would print.

- The MEJT sequence featured an ultimate sell signal (**MEJT**), an ultimate buy signal (**MEJT+1**) and a **MEJT+2** bar which closed within the MEJT range. The system called for higher and lower prices and marked the afternoon rally as unsustainable.

Result

It would have been difficult to profit from the am ultimate buy signal. The market closed over the high of the three-bar range pretty quickly. But traders did have the potential to profit by fading the afternoon rally, which the system said would not stick.

Day 10

Figure 9.10 – 12 January 2010

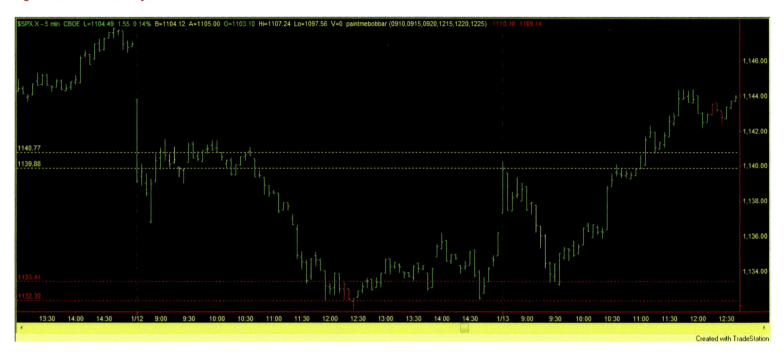

As can be seen in Figure 9.10, 12 January started with a sizeable drop and the **am+1** ultimate sell signal said more downside was coming. However both **am+2** and MEJT+2 signalled that, ultimately, higher prices would print.

MEJT+2 closed in its upper half and within the MEJT range. This signalled that the **MEJT** low (1132.41) should be undercut before a sustainable move could begin.

Result

Ultimately, the market did trade over the highs of the **am MEJT** and **MEJT** sequences. The afternoon rally began from a low of 1132.44, which is within the 0.20 tolerance for the 1132.41- target. Reversals within that range usually run into resistance no more than eight to ten points higher, but this rally went for more than that. Even though 1132.41- (undercutting the **MEJT** low) was no longer a required target, it usually prints anyway, so it would pay to write it down as an optional target. Eventually, it did print.

Day 11

Figure 9.11 – 13 January 2010

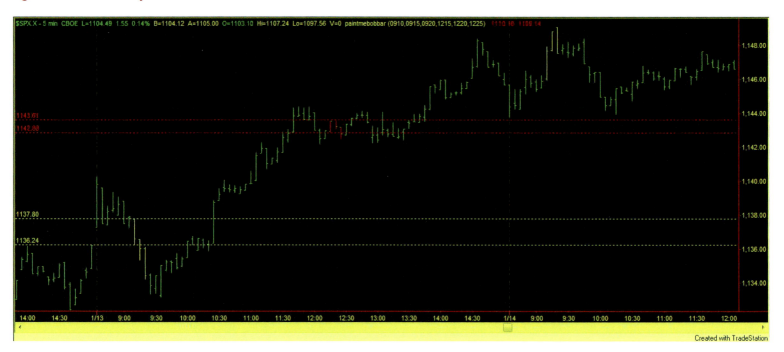

- The unfilled gap left us with no signal from the morning.

- The **MEJT+1** and **MEJT+2** bars did not attempt to trend.

Result

As predicted, S&P 500 traded over and under **MEJT** and waited an hour before making its move.

Day 12

Figure 9.12 – 14 January 2010

- The gap filled, but an ultimate sell signal from **am+2** indicated the rally attempt was not for keeps and that, ultimately, lower prices would print.

- **MEJT+1** and **MEJT+2** both went nowhere. With no attempt to trend and with **MEJT+2** closing within the MEJT range, the rules said the afternoon rally was doomed to retrace.

- A **MEJT+3** buy signal was given.

Result

The **am+2** ultimate sell signal paid off immediately, making it untradable if the MEJT rules were all one was using. However, the morning drop came too soon according to the time criteria and, without support from the am sequence, it could not stick; the rules justified fading the decline, which would have been profitable. The **MEJT+3** buy signal worked. The MEJT sequence call for a retracement. It worked – and worked well – by the next morning.

Day 13

Figure 9.13 – 15 January 2010

The unfilled gap meant there was no am signal, but the **am+2** ultimate buy signal predicted that, ultimately, the market would rally – ideally over the high of the three bar **am MEJT** sequence.

MEJT+2 closed within the range of **MEJT** and in its lower half as well. The rules told us that the strong rally that ensued began too soon and without prices moving lower than the **MEJT** bar. That gave us a target of 1132.48-.

Result

By the next day the market had recovered over the am sequence high. Prices did not undercut the **MEJT** low within the preferred time frame (the following day), but did satisfy the target soon thereafter.

Day 14

Figure 9.14 – 19 January 2010

When the range of the first bar of the day nicks the close of the prior day, one cannot rely on figures from S&P 500 alone to decide if a gap is present. The reason is that all components of the index do not open simultaneously. Thus, the slight overlap seen in this example could be an artefact created by the staggered opens of various index constituents.

The proper technique in such a situation is to look at the prices of futures or SPY, the exchange traded fund which tracks S&P 500. SPY closed 15 January at 113.64 and changed hands 19 January, the next day of trading, as low as 113.62. Thus there was no gap and the **am MEJT** buy signal counted.

MEJT gave an ultimate buy signal. **MEJT+2** closed in its lower half and within the **MEJT** range, predicting the afternoon rally would retrace.

Result

The buy signals from the am sequence and the MEJT ultimate buy signal were satisfied. By the next day, the market had undercut the **MEJT** low just as the rules called for.

This day marked a significant market high. There was marked complacency as shown by the volatility index being at a yearly low; this is a characteristic of a market top. This day's MEJT signal was further justification for shorting the market.

Day 15

Figure 9.15 – 20 January 2010

Created with TradeStation

The unfilled gap meant no am signal.

The MEJT sequence gave no support for the afternoon rally, so the rules required it to retrace. MEJT closed at 1130.72. This was under the MEJT low of 1130.73, so the retracement required prices to return to the MEJT high and not to undercut the low. As was obvious by the next morning, this target was a minimum target.

Result

The signals worked. The afternoon rally did not stick and traders who shorted that move were well rewarded by the next morning.

Day 16

Figure 9.16 – 21 January 2010

- The gap filled, so the **am MEJT** signal counted.

- **Am+2** closed in its upper half and did not take out a significant level. The rules suggested that the decline should not stick and targeted a return to the **am** low, 1138.89.

- The MEJT sequence met the criteria for a sustainable advance.

Result

This is an example of what I call a failed target. Anyone who bought based on the signal and did not use a stop would have been seriously hurt.

I considered calling targets which did not print in their preferred time frame *delayed* rather than *failed*, but I didn't – if it is my money on the line the prediction is a failure. I am intentionally including this example to illustrate that, even with a good system like MEJT, it is important to use stops and money management. The target printed eventually, validating the call well outside its preferred time frame.

There was a rally that satisfied the MEJT signal. The weak close of **MEJT+1** suggested subsequent market action may be weak as well; this information justified taking a quick scalp profit for anyone who acted on the signal.

Index

preferred time

    am sequence 18, 24

    pm sequence 8, 71

prior relative extreme 68, 72, 73, 74

prior relative high 68

prior relative low 68

profit forecast 36

R

reference bar 8, 117

    defining, in am sequence 18, 20-1

    defining, in pm sequence 70,

resistance

    covert 133, 134

    overt 133

reversal bar 107

    outside 107

    variant 107

S

S&P 500

    daily trading pattern 17

    predictability of afternoon trading 67

significant level

    taking out 24, 28

support

    covert 133, 134

    overt 133

swing high 68

swing low 68

T

targets 32-3

    consolidations, from 119

    examples 122-30

    failed (postponed) 45, 71, 120-1

      example of 179

    no swing extreme nearby 119

    optional 117

required 117

sustainable moves 118-19

ultimate signals 120

unsustainable moves 117-18

technical analysis 5, 107

use other techniques in combination with MEJT 147

TradeStation 9, 147

Fibonacci grid, use of to create a 133

use of alternative software, in place of 11

using to indentify the bars of the am and pm sequence 9-10

trends

delayed 24, 27, 71, 72

immediate 24, 27, 71, 72

sustainable 7-8, 19-20, 73

examples

am sequence 24-5, 29, 31

pm sequence 81, 83-4, 125, 129, 154-5, 178-9

unsustainable 19, 28, 73

examples

am sequence 26, 42, 43, 45, 122-3, 125, 150-1, 156-7

pm sequence 75, 80, 83-4, 126-7, 150-1, 164-5

strong 27, 72

weak 27, 72

U

ultimate buy or sell signal 107

examples 108-114